Grant Teaff

with Louis and Kay Moore

WINNING

It's How You Play the Game

WORD BOOKS
PUBLISHER
WACO, TEXAS

A DIVISION OF
WORD, INCORPORATED

Library of Congress Cataloging in Publication Data

Teaff, Grant, 1933–
    1. Football—Coaching.   2. Motivation (Psychology)
I. Moore, Louis.   II. Moore, Kay.   III. Title.
GV956.6.T43   1985   796.332′07′7   85–16722
ISBN 0–8499–0520–6

Printed in the United States of America

56789FG987654321

To: *Speedy Moffatt, Mule Kizer,* and *Tommy Bean,* who represent the junior high and high school coaches, who inspired me to become a coach.

To: *Wilfred Moore, Tommy Ellis,* and *Max Bumgardner,* who literally taught me how to play the game of football, and represent all my college coaches.

To: *Cap Shelton, Jack Patterson,* and *Vernon Hilliard,* who represent all the coaches who shared their knowledge with a young, aspiring track coach.

To: *J. T. King, John Conley,* and *Phil George,* who represent all the coaches who believed in me as a football coach.

To: *Pete Shotwell, Chuck Moser,* and *John Clark,* who represent all of the high school coaches who set a standard in our profession.

To: *Gordon Wood, George Kirk,* and *Bob McQueen,* who represent the hundreds of high school coaches who have not only shared their knowledge with me, but their players as well.

To: *Hershel Kimbrell, Buddy Fornes,* and *Bill Lane,* who represent all of the coaches, who have so faithfully shared my opportunities, my goals, and my philosophy.

And finally, to the men and women in our profession, who serve the youth of America, now and in the future.

WINNING

1

Winning Is . . .
More Than Not Losing

Winning

To a football coach, that one word is the most important in all the English language. It summarizes a coach's entire mission in life. It is the goal that keeps the adrenalin flowing throughout the frustrations of spring training. It keeps the spirits up during day after day of exhausting workouts. It becomes the single purpose that propels us during the grueling fall football season.

Seeing that scoreboard lit up at the end of a game with my team on top makes everything worth it all. I experienced this in 1974 in a way that few other college football coaches ever will. That was the year Baylor University won its first Southwest Conference championship in more than fifty years.

With this win, the eyes of the nation turned on Baylor University and the school achieved a long-overdue honor and recognition. I was elected National Coach of the Year and received coaching awards from nearly every sports organization in the country. Just the year before, our team had emerged with a 2–9 record and we were in the valley of despair. The triumph 1974 brought after that nightmare just the previous season made us feel like winners in every sense of the word.

After that triumph, I wrote the book *I Believe* with sports writer Sam Blair. This allowed me to share the winning story

11

of Baylor University and my personal Christian testimony with people all over the United States.

Although that final tally is crucial, it is certainly not the most important part of winning. The kind of winning I'm talking about goes far beyond the numbers on the scoreboard. It is the type of winning that reaches down into the very core of one's being. It is the type of winning that can occur no matter how lonely or dejected one feels—no matter how run over someone is by life's circumstances. It is the kind of winning that this book is really about.

More Than Just Football Strategies

I'm not writing here about football strategies or ways to make a team Number 1 in the national standings, although I believe that some of the comments on motivation here can inspire others to great achievements. This book is designed to give some new perspectives on winning that far transcend those numbers the sports writers will use in Sunday's papers to describe what happened on the Saturday playing fields.

Whenever I think about this kind of winning, I think about Philip Kent.

When Philip Kent first arrived at Baylor University in the spring of 1973, he seemed to start out like a real loser. He had signed on with Baylor University out of Tyler Junior College and moved to Waco with his young family, which consisted of his wife Jan, his daughter Peaches and his baby son Bubba. Philip was full of hopes and dreams when he arrived at Baylor University, and he was so eager to do well that I found myself hoping that every one of his dreams would come true.

Philip had enjoyed good, solid success at Tyler Junior College and was determined to become a starter with Baylor University instantly, since he had only two years of eligibility left.

But almost immediately after beginning spring practice, Philip injured himself and could not go full speed. He could not achieve his goal of making the starting lineup. I'm sure Philip thought things would be better in the fall of 1973. They were not. Philip hurt his knee and missed the whole season.

Time and time again I remember Philip standing on the sidelines beside me holding the wires to my headset and pulling for his teammates on the field. He wanted so badly to do something with his life but was held back because of his injury.

The fact that our team was doing poorly in 1973 made Philip feel even worse and even more powerless. Game after game in 1973, we lost in the fourth quarter by very few points. Philip suffered through those defeats in a big way. He was beginning to wonder if he would ever taste victory of any kind again.

Soon 1973 was past history and 1974 was a fresh clean slate. Beginning in January, 1974, I began telling our team and coaching staff what I felt we must do with defeat, and Philip was right there listening to it all.

I told the players that we must take defeat, slam it to the ground, step on it and rise above it, using it as a stepping stone to victory. The question was asked, "How do you slam defeat to the ground?" My answer came quickly. "By exercising your faith you can ultimately overcome defeat in life and become a winner." I told them that believing in those things yet unseen and unproven, by putting one's faith in God allows us to believe in ourselves and have faith in others. I told them we must believe that we are winners, capable of being happy and victorious and successful.

After one of those sessions, Philip shared with me that he and Jan had been Christians for a long time. He told me they talked often about their own faith—their faith in God, their faith in themselves, their faith in what they were doing at Baylor University and their faith in what they were trying to accomplish. He said that at one point recently, they evaluated their lives and decided that their faith had been superficial, so they made a recommitment of their lives to God, believing He would give them the faith they needed for their goals.

Fortunately, Philip Kent, along with the rest of the Baylor Bears, had a chance to become winners in 1974.

After a great spring training, Philip became our starting wing back for his senior year. When the season started in 1974, Philip was the big play man. Game after game he contributed long yardage and was a great receiver. He helped win the games that eventually gave Baylor University its first Southwest Conference championship in more than fifty years, a berth in the Cotton Bowl and national recognition. Victory after victory came in all of our lives. The pain and frustration of our 2–9 season in 1973 diminished before us as we became winners in the eyes of the world.

Philip Kent changed his own personal status as a loser in a big way. He graduated from Baylor University and was drafted by the Miami Dolphins. Knowing that Philip had made a recommitment to Christ, I could see a real difference in everything about the way he lived his life. Just before he took off for Miami, he accepted an invitation to play in the All-America game in June, 1975, a game I had been asked to coach.

I always chuckle a little when I think of a funny line Philip told me one morning when we were in Lubbock working out for the All-Star game. Just before the workout, I asked him about his children. I was especially fond of little four-year-old Peaches. She used to come to the football workouts in her little Baylor t-shirt and run up and down the sidelines, her little black pigtails flying in the breeze. She would be yelling for her daddy and the Baylor Bears.

When I inquired about his youngsters back home in Houston, Philip said he had talked to them just that morning and that little Peaches had said to tell Coach Teaff "hello" and she hoped the Baylor Bears won. I said, "Phil, doesn't she know that this is an All-Star game?" He said, "Coach, she thinks anybody that you're coaching and I'm playing for couldn't be anything but the Baylor Bears."

Emotional Good-byes

Philip played a great game for me in that All-Star contest. Down in the dressing room after the game was over, it was an emotional time since I was bidding all those great players good-bye as they departed for their new pro football assignments. I walked around and shook hands with various ones—our Baylor University quarterback that year, Neal Jeffrey, who was leaving to go to the San Diego Chargers and who later went on to be a Baptist minister working with youth, and Derrel Luce as he was heading out to go to the Baltimore Colts and later would become a successful lawyer in Waco.

But the most emotional good-bye of all came when I walked to the end of the dressing room and saw Philip Kent standing there in the darkness. We didn't shake hands. We just fell into each others' arms and held each other tightly. Philip said, "I can't tell you how much I love you, Coach, and how much Baylor University has meant to me." And I said, "Phil, you've been an inspiration to us all. You know I love you and I always will. I want you to know that though you are no longer associated with Baylor as a player, I love and care about you and our relationship will never diminish. If there's ever anything that you need, pick up the telephone and call me collect."

When I made that suggestion, I was actually thinking about his new career as a pro football player and how difficult it is to make it in the pros. Aspirations are so high. When players fail to do well, the hurt is deep and they need someone to understand. I wanted him to know that I was available to him in this new phase of his young life.

Little did I realize that on Wednesday of the next week I would be on the phone with Philip in a time of need far different from what I had envisioned. I would see Philip as a winner in a way that far exceeded any I had known in him previously.

When I picked up the phone that day and heard Philip's quivering voice, he was calling to break the dreadful news that his beautiful daughter Peaches had just died on the operating table. While undergoing some minor cosmetic surgery, her little heart stopped unexpectedly. Shocked, stunned and brokenhearted at this revelation, I asked Philip what I could do. He said he would appreciate it very much if I would come to Houston. I flew there the next morning. Someone picked me up at the airport and brought me to Philip's granddad's home. All the way to Houston and all the way across town, I prayed fervently for God to give me the words to say to this young couple in this unbelievable time of need.

When I arrived, Philip was waiting for me on the porch. As I walked up to him, I gritted my teeth and prayed again, "O God, give me the words to say." As my eyes met Philip's, tears started streaming down our cheeks. I could not speak. I walked inside and saw Jan. I held her tightly for a few moments, still unable to speak.

I heard Bubba come running into the room from the back of the house. He was asking for his little playmate Peaches, unable to comprehend that she had gone away, never to return. My heart was in my throat. I ached all over. I knew that somehow, some way we had to talk. I motioned for Philip and Jan to go into the adjoining bedroom. I closed the door behind us. The two of them sat on the bed and I pulled a chair up close. Again, I was praying, "O God, give me the words."

Rising above Every Defeat

But before I could utter a sound, Jan said to me, "Coach, we appreciate your coming here more than you will ever know, and we'd like to ask you to do something very special for us."

I said, "Yes, you name it and it will be done." Jan said, "Coach, we'd like for you to help officiate in Peaches' funeral on Saturday." Without hesitation, I agreed.

Then, before I could utter another word, Jan went on to say, "Coach, there's something else that we want you to know. We're going to overcome this defeat. We're going to literally slam it into the ground, step on it and rise above it. We're not going to let it hang around our neck like a yoke and pull us down and destroy us. There is a void and a vacuum in our lives where little Peaches was, and there always will be, but we're not going to let this defeat destroy our lives and Bubba's." Then Philip added, "Coach, we want you to know that the only way we could do this is through our faith. That's the only way. Faith will see us through it."

I had gone to Houston to try to help two young people whom I loved, but instead, their inspiration and their words taught me the greatest lesson about winning that I'll ever learn. You can take all the football games that have ever been lost and put them in a pile and they're microscopic compared to the loss of our Peaches.

And yet despite this defeat, Philip and Jan are winners. They understand the importance of faith in their lives. They have made good on their promise to rise above their loss. Today, Philip Kent owns his own automobile business in Houston. He and Jan have three sons and, yes, a new baby daughter. They are the same devoted, faithful Christians they were before this tragedy struck in their lives. Their faith was not shaken by this terrible loss. They were truly winners in every sense of the word, no matter what the scoreboard of their lives showed. Faith, as they assured me back then, did see them through.

This is the type of winning this book is all about.

2

Winning Is . . .
Not Letting the Odds Stand in Your Way

The excitement and anticipation of the 1975 season was almost frightening in light of what we'd just accomplished. The Baylor alumni, students, and fans were unanimous in their cries of "Let's do it again. Let's make it two in a row" for the conference championship.

I thought to myself, *Why not?* We had an excellent preseason period of workouts. There were high expectations among our coaching staff and certainly among the players. The determination was there, and the right attitudes seemed to prevail. We seemed to be in a perfect frame of mind for a repeat performance of our victorious 1974 year.

We opened by playing a well-known team in college football circles—the Ole Miss Rebels, a great football powerhouse in years gone by and still a very respected group. We incorporated a power attack against Ole Miss and won the game 14–10.

Then came our second home game in a row, again with a very good Southeast Conference football team—Auburn University. This was Coach Shug Jordan's last year to be the Auburn coach. He'd had a very successful tenure and would be replaced by Doug Barfield, who had been Jordan's offensive coordinator. The game meant a lot to me personally because we had just defeated one Southeast Conference team. The chance to defeat another would be a tremendous boost to our program. It would give us a position of strength early on as we went into the rest of the season.

The Auburn-Baylor match turned out to be an excellent ball game, with the final score 10–10. Even a slight question raised by some Alabama sports writers about a Baylor field goal in the closing seconds of the first half could not detract from our tie with Auburn. The field goal began with ten seconds showing on the clock at the end of the first half. We had practiced this kick hundreds of times in workouts. We called it our "nine-second field goal."

Our field goal team was poised and ready on the sideline. With ten seconds left to go in the first half, I sent them onto the field. They sprinted on without a huddle, the ball was snapped with about three seconds to go and the kick was up and in the air as the buzzer sounded.

Those three points contributed heavily to the final score of the game. Naturally, many of the sports writers in Alabama were highly critical of our score. We knew we were in the right, and we were thrilled to be undefeated against two Southeast Conference foes. We did not let their nit-picking deter us.

The next week we played the University of Michigan in Ann Arbor. The crowd was predicted to be more than 106,000, the largest audience Baylor University had ever played before. In fact, it was the third largest crowd in the history of college football at that time.

Bo Schembechler, the head football coach at Michigan, had had some tremendous successes in his time there. Michigan was particularly strong on its home field, playing always before sell-out crowds. As I looked at the game film, studying the Michigan offense and the defense, I discovered one thing that I felt helped Michigan to be so effective on its home field. Michigan used good psychology and intimidated its opponents. This was an important discovery for us.

The Importance of Mental Preparation

To be successful on and off the football field, I believe that a team has to prepare mentally; therefore, at Baylor University, we spend the same amount of time in preparing mentally as we do physically. It is a misconception that a team gets ready mentally right before the game. In truth, a team only executes during a ball game that which it has prepared all week to do. There is a definite way of preparing physically and a definite way of preparing mentally for a game.

Our mental preparation for the week begins with a Monday morning staff meeting where our coaching staff does a lot of brainstorming. We review the previous week's game and evaluate the pluses and minuses of our team's attitude. Then we discuss what kind of attitude it will take to win the next game. Once we reach a decision, we adopt a theme for the week, which we will then try to communicate to our players. We do this by developing a special word for each day of the practice week which will reinforce the theme. The "word of the day" is written on the message board so that all players will see it as they enter the dressing room. Then, the offensive and defensive coordinators take the word of the day and talk about it from their own experiences. The position coaches do the same thing. At the end of each day when practice is over, I call the team together and I talk about the "word for the day," explaining it by drawing from my own experiences. This procedure is followed on Monday through Thursday of each week.

On the Thursday prior to the Michigan game, I made an unusual revelation to our players. Our word for that day was "poise." As I talked about the importance of poise in being successful and winning football games, I told them that I had discovered why Michigan was so intimidating on its home field. Michigan had won 37 of its last 38 ball games on its home field. I had observed that Michigan would allow the opponents to come onto this football field prior to the kickoff. Then, the Michigan team would rush onto the field. Those 100,000-plus fans would stand and give their team a resounding ovation with screams and yells and shouts to emphasize how much they supported their players. The opponents, meanwhile, who were usually from some far-flung state and without large groups of fans in the stands, became psychologically intimidated at this overwhelming noise. You could almost see the opponents on the field beginning to shrivel and shrink into submission.

Our players all became very hushed as I revealed all this to them. I told them that we could use this information to help us against Michigan, but the only way we could do it was to go into that stadium poised, with a plan in mind that would help us offset Michigan's advantage.

According to the plan I had devised, we would go into the stadium, take our regular warmups, go back to our dressing room, shut the door and finish all of our preparatory business prior to going down on the field. Then we would turn the lights down low and I would turn on some soft stereo music for the players to listen to, and we would absolutely not go on to the field before Michigan made its entrance. I warned the players again that the only way we could successfully pull it off would be to be under complete control emotionally—to be poised and to be ready to sit in that dressing room for an hour if we had to.

The faces of the players lit up as the wheels in their minds began to turn and they could envision themselves pulling a fast one on Michigan right in the home team's own stadium.

Then I heard a voice come from the back of the room saying, "Let's do it, Coach. Let's do it." I warned the players, "When you get before those 106,000 people up there, you're going to be chomping at the bit to get on the football field and to play Michigan. You'll fall right into the trap. We must be prepared to go into the dressing room, sit down, listen to some soft music and stay until Michigan goes on the field."

"Yeah, yeah," they continued to insist. "Let's do it."

As the days went by before our Michigan game, we perfected and fine-tuned our plan. On Saturday afternoon as our players warmed up, I walked around the field looking each of them in the eyes. As we made eye contact, I winked at each individual player and he winked back at me. We knew something the other team did not know. It would totally foul up Michigan's plans to intimidate the Baylor Bears.

Then we went back to our dressing room. It seemed literally to be half a block under the stands although it was probably less than fifty yards. Our dressing room was on the right; Michigan's was directly across the hall on the left. Walking into that dressing room, you could almost see the ghosts of all the great players who had suited out in this room and had then gone out to do battle against the Michigan Wolverines in the many years that this powerhouse team had played in this stadium. I smiled to myself a little as I realized how many of them had been devastated by these next few minutes of pregame play. I felt a little smug because I knew that the Baylor Bears would not fall victim to this humiliation today.

A Plan That Worked

Then we began to execute our strategy. We briefly reviewed our game plan offensively and defensively. Someone offered the final team prayer. Then, as players lifted their heads from praying, the stereo was turned on with some quiet music. Each player and each coach found himself a spot in the dressing room and sank back into a comfortable position, waiting while the lights were dimmed.

Seconds ticked by, then minutes, and then all of a sudden the door to the dressing room slowly opened. A head appeared in the doorway. It was the referee. "Coach Teaff!" he called. "Coach Teaff!"

"I'm right over here in the corner," I replied.

"It's time to get out on the field immediately," he yelled.

Calmly I replied, "Mr. Referee, we will come on the field after Michigan is on."

"What?" he asked in disbelief.

"We will go on the field after Michigan takes the field, Mr. Referee," I said, repeating myself.

"You can't do that. You've got to go now," he said, almost barking.

I told him, "There's nothing in our contract that says we have to go onto the field at any particular time. I'm telling you right now, we will be on the field immediately after Michigan takes the field."

The door closed. I could hear him walk away and immediately go to the other dressing room. I could hear shouts coming from across the hall. Michigan was obviously excited and ready to play, but Baylor would not go on the field first.

The referee came back and the door popped open again. He stuck his head in to say, "Coach Teaff, you've got to go on the field."

I replied, "We're not going. Please do not bother us again. We're here listening to some great music. We're relaxed and comfortable. Please leave us alone."

From across the room, I could hear snickers from both players and coaches. The door closed again. Suddenly, we could hear a huge noise of yelling, screaming, the slamming of helmets against the door and then finally the clicking of the cleats as Michigan moved out into the tunnel. At last I turned to our players and said, "Men, it's time to go." We got up immediately, opened the door, pulled on our caps and our helmets and came right out behind the Michigan players, ready to play.

When Michigan hit the field in front of us, the much-awaited roar began, just as we had anticipated. One of our coaches in the press box later told us that the players and coaches from Michigan emerged with their hands in a palms-up fashion, indicating that they didn't know what had happened to the Baylor Bears, but they had just come on anyway. What they didn't know was that we had slipped out right behind them. We had the sensation that the crowd was roaring for us, too. We also had the incredible feeling of realizing that we had just pulled a good one on the University of Michigan team.

Our football team played like the take-charge group that it was that day, too. We moved the football up and down the field from one end to the other. We scored first, then Michigan scored, and we scored again. Then we drove to the six-yard line. We ran the quarterback to the right and he was knocked out of bounds on the one-inch line. Michigan took over. Michigan scored and tied the score 14–14. The Bears, with seconds left, missed a field goal from the seven-yard line.

We won what looked to everyone like a moral victory. The mighty Michigan team did not trounce us as the news media predicted. They only managed to conclude the game in a tie. Our tailback that day made 139 yards against a very good Michigan team. We moved up and down the field and everyone realized that we outplayed Michigan and should have won the football game. I feel very strongly that our mental preparation and the psychological advantage which we gained by that preparation were instrumental in the kind of football game we played and the end results.

Nevertheless, the tie was actually no victory at all to our football team and our coaching staff. The fact remained that even though we were undefeated in 1975 through three games, our wins still amounted to only one.

Some Interesting Attention

An amusing sequel to the Michigan game happened the following Monday. Most of the coaches in the United States have a

Woody Hayes story, and now I have mine as well. As I came out of a staff meeting that morning, my secretary told me that I had a message to immediately call Coach Woody Hayes of Ohio State University. I took the number, walked into the office and dialed this legendary coach forthwith, wondering as I dialed what could have prompted his call.

Coach Hayes answered the telephone. I said, "Coach Hayes, this is Grant Teaff returning your call."

"Oh, Grant, great to hear from you!" he said. "I want to talk with you about your game with Michigan. Now, you guys did a great job. I would like for you to explain to me exactly what you were doing to Michigan for your tailback to make all that yardage. You made a lot of yardage on them. Now tell me, exactly what were you doing?"

I told Coach Hayes that we had a simple plan. We used a lead play out of the "I" formation, and we read the defensive player lined up closest to our offensive guard. In other words, if the defensive player moved to our right, we just took him to our right; if he moved to our left, we took him to our left. We let our fullback then read the offensive guard's block and the tailback would follow the fullback wherever he went. It made a very simplified play that would hit either inside or outside the offensive guard, based on the movement of the defense.

As I talked, Coach Hayes became more and more excited about this play and had me go over each phase of it again in minute detail. We talked for an hour. Finally as we concluded our conversation, Coach Hayes asked for the film of the Michigan game. He wanted to make a copy of it and mail it right back. I thought for a moment and then said, "Coach Hayes, what do you think Coach Schembechler would think about that?" He shot right back, "What do you mean? Bo's got his own copy of the film. He's been studying it too." Needless to say, I fired the film off to Coach Hayes that afternoon.

A Call That Spelled Crisis

But another call I got that day ended on less than a humorous note. Someone at Waco High School called to inform me that a sixteen-year-old freshman had been involved in an accident on the football field. He had been working out for football. He tried to make a tackle and his neck was broken. He had been

rushed to the hospital and placed in intensive care. Representatives from the school asked if I could come and talk to his family,
and of course I agreed. I drove to the hospital. When I arrived
there, I found that the youngster, Anthony Cervantes, had indeed
broken his neck and damaged his spinal cord. There was a question at that point as to whether he would even live. I visited
his mother and found out that he was one of many children
and that the parents were separated. The mother naturally was
scared, concerned and bewildered. I did not get to see Anthony
at that time but I promised I would come back to see him and
do what I could to encourage and to help him. I also found
out from talking to Mrs. Cervantes that there would be a financial
problem because of lack of insurance.

I left the hospital and started driving back to my office. I
had only driven about two blocks when all of a sudden I was
overwhelmed by emotion. I could do nothing but pull to the
side of the road and begin to cry for the sixteen-year-old whom
I had just left at the hospital. Anthony was not only fighting
for his life but he was fighting for the mere semblance of normalcy
that he faced if he lived. I cried for a scared and concerned
family, horrified at the prospects of what lay ahead of him. I
asked myself what could I do. But then I realized that I already
had done something, and I had done it as God worked through
me. I realized that the thing that Christ had placed in me—
love of my fellow man—had emerged in this situation. I did
not know the young man, had never even seen his face but yet
I felt an immeasurable love and deep concern for him. I had
asked myself what I could do to help. I could simply try to
help motivate Anthony as he moved into rehabilitation. I could
help in the area of encouragement. And yes, I could help even
beyond that. Suddenly I knew that there was even more that I
could do. And I knew it had to be done.

A familiar creed came to my mind: "That which I can do, I
ought to do. That which I ought to do by God's grace I will
do." At that moment, I pledged myself to go the last mile helping
this young man and his family.

When I got back to the office, I immediately called in our
coaching staff and informed them of Anthony's circumstances.
Later that afternoon, I informed our players. They also committed
themselves to helping Anthony. They promised that they would

write letters. They pledged to give a game ball to Anthony and a jersey with a special number that would make him an official member of the Baylor University football team. Our coaches pledged to help in any way they could financially, but I knew that what we could do as a coaching staff and as a team would still not be enough.

The next morning I talked to the Waco High School administration and asked them how I could help. A few days later they assigned me to head up a rehabilitation fund for Anthony Cervantes. We set up a trust fund and began to lay the plans for helping to raise money for this young man. I thought that my television show, which at that time was fed into seventeen markets in Texas and surrounding states, would be a good forum for soliciting help for Anthony. We cut some spots to be used on the television show and set up a method of appeal.

In the meantime I had visited several times with Anthony himself and had gotten to know him personally. I was very impressed with him. He had a beautiful face and a warm smile, even though his eyes were filled with doubts and concern and fear. On every visit, I always urged him to keep a positive attitude.

But on the day he was to leave for Carruth Rehabilitation Center in Dallas, I felt it was time to tell him what we had in mind in the way of a rehabilitation fund. I said to him, "Anthony, you're going to be seeing on television, reading in the newspapers and hearing about a fund that is being started to help you and your family during your rehabilitation time. I just wanted you to know what we are doing."

Anthony's reaction startled me a little. He looked at me with pleading eyes and said, "Coach, please don't do this. Please don't."

Bewildered, I asked, "Anthony, why?"

He said, "Coach, no one will help me. No one will help in any way. You'll see. You'll be disappointed. No one will help."

I looked Anthony straight in the eye, and I said, "Anthony, you're wrong. People will be happy to help."

He said, "No, Coach. No one will help."

But thankfully, Anthony was wrong in every way. We started the Anthony Cervantes fund through television. Area high schools pitched in and young people started to work to help Anthony. In two weeks' time, we had accumulated $10,000.00.

On a Friday before a ball game, I took two of our players to Dallas with me to see Anthony. We went in and visited and encouraged him for a while.

After the players handed him the game ball and the jersey that they had promised him and left the room, I stayed behind. Leaning over Anthony and looking down into his face, I said, "Anthony, before I go I want to share something with you. You know the fund that I told you about?"

"Yes sir," he replied. "I saw it on television."

Then I told him the good news. "I just want you to know that in a little more than two weeks, we have collected more than $10,000.00 to help you and your family."

Suddenly, his eyes began to fill with tears. As he lay flat on his back, the tears began to trickle from the corners of his eyes and down his face and onto his pillow.

I said, "Anthony, aren't you happy?"

He replied, "Oh, yes, Coach, I'm very happy. I just can't believe it, that's all."

"What can't you believe?" I asked him.

He said, "I can't understand why anyone would give me money. They don't know me. Why would they help?"

"Anthony, they gave because they care," I said. "They love you even though they don't know you. They're showing their love by their action of giving."

I'll never forget what Anthony said then. Looking straight into my eyes, he said, "Coach, if all of those people love me, surely God must love me, too."

The money for Anthony did not stop but continued on for weeks afterward, and Anthony continued to improve. He still cannot walk, but Anthony lives a vibrant life today. There's no question in my mind that part of his positive attitude now is because people cared enough to help back then. Love motivates against all odds.

Injuries Cripple the Baylor Bears

The early fortunes of the 1975 football season tumbled as critical injuries began to crop up among many of our players. In football, there is an old maxim that says, "If you lose your starting quarterback, you will lose most of the games that season." That maxim was never more true for Baylor University than in 1975. Starting quarterback Mark Jackson hurt his shoulder and was out for two full weeks. He came back, played the rest of the season but was hampered tremendously because of the injury.

The low point of the 1975 season came when we played Arkansas in Baylor Stadium before a very good crowd. Arkansas beat us badly. One of the fans was heard to remark as he left the stadium that night, "Ole Grant needs to write another book. He needs to call this one, *Would You Believe?*" Little did that fan know he was summing up my own feelings about the entire 1975 season in very appropriate words.

That season, it helped me a great deal to remember the old saying, "If you won't be beaten, you can't be beaten." It probably could have been rephrased, "If you won't give up even when you are beaten, it won't destroy you." There's tremendous power in having the feeling that you're not going to be devastated by circumstances and that you will not give up, come what may. You may get knocked down time and time again, but you'll get back up on your feet and continue to fight. Never give up!

3

Winning Is . . .
Fighting One More Round

The 1976 season at Baylor University was one of the most rewarding of my coaching career. I had the joy of working with a group of seniors who had taken part in a tremendous range of football experiences during their four years in college. They had known the whole gamut of emotions that one experiences in competition—the disgrace of defeat and then the thrill of victory beyond anyone's expectations and imagination. They were part of a championship team (the first in more than fifty years at Baylor University, as I've already mentioned) and they literally changed Baylor's image from that of a loser to that of a winner.

Then, in 1975, that team had remained champions in its spirit and performance even though it was not in the cards for the team to win a repeat championship. However, I believe this team's senior and final year was its finest hour.

Going into this season we felt, as did the sports writing community, that Baylor University had an outside chance of winning another championship. Our team exuded an air of confidence about being winners.

We opened the season against the University of Houston, welcoming the Cougars for the first time as competitors in the Southwest Conference. The game was to be played in Baylor Stadium and was to be televised regionally.

On Thursday afternoon before that fateful Saturday, we were

on the practice field working out. It was a day of sweat suits, helmets, running through the kicking game and polishing the offense and the defense as we had done many times before.

As we polished the kicking game, an onside kick was simulated. The receiving team, our offensive team, was to go to the ball and position itself around it in gamelike manner without falling on the ball.

For some unexplained reason, our starting right tackle, who was a senior and had been a starter for four years, left the ground and flew through the air toward the ball. Standing close by was Ron Barnes, our starting center.

As the tackle dove for the ball, he smashed into Barnes' leg and shattered it. The television crew, setting up equipment for the coming Saturday game, looked down to see a paralyzed football team and a coaching staff scrambling to aid a young man with a horribly broken leg. A blanket of gloom fell on that practice field for more reasons than one. Not only did the accident mean an injury to a young man who wanted to play, it also meant the Baylor Bears were out of offensive centers. A second center, senior Billy Wayne Clements, had hurt his knee two weeks prior to this time and could not work out. With Barnes' injury, we were out of candidates for this crucial position.

We moved a freshman tackle, Arland Thompson, into the slot. He had played center in the Texas High School All-Star Game and that, plus a small bit of experience while a sophomore in high school, was his total background as a center. Now Thompson was starting for Baylor University against the University of Houston.

Not only did we have these injuries, but we had also lost our starting tailback, Cleveland Franklin, a leading rusher on our squad and one of the great running backs in the nation. He had injured his knee.

With all these strikes against us, it was no wonder that Houston, enthusiastic because of its opportunity to play in the conference for the first time, ended up winning the ball game.

The Loss That Didn't Destroy Us

Losing our first game, especially when it was a conference match and in our own stadium as well, could have completely destroyed our season—that is, if we had not had the power within us not to give up. Instead of letting our team feel sorry for itself, we coaches became more intense and more hard-nosed. Rather than showing sympathy about our loss, we built intensity toward our upcoming game against Auburn University.

When our plane arrived at Auburn, Alabama, we were anticipating a victory, partly because we had spent just as much time in mental preparation as we had in physical preparation for the football game. Part of this mental preparation was positive visualization—deliberately imagining positive situations that will happen in a ball game. We had done this throughout the week before the Auburn game, and we did it again in the dressing room at Auburn Stadium just prior to the match. Our players were taped, dressed and waiting for the game to start. Then I asked each player to close his eyes and to try to imagine the situations in which we would soon find ourselves on the athletic field that day.

Visualize What the Problems May Be

For example, I asked them to visualize themselves in a spot where our defense would have its back to the wall and it would look like the whole football season was about to crumble. This was, in fact, realistic. Another loss, on top of the one to Houston at the beginning of the season, would have been disastrous. Instead of being horrified at this thought, I asked the players to think about the good things that might happen, that in this clutch position we would be able to do exactly the right thing to stop Auburn University. I told them to visualize themselves not giving up and winning despite all odds.

"There will come a time," I said, "when we will find our backs against the wall. Someone must reach down and do whatever is necessary to stop Auburn University. From an Auburn running back we're going to recover a fumble and change the whole complexion of the ball game." I also said, "Visualize this. We're down by one touchdown. We must drive the length of the football field to win. We're going to score, go for two and win the game. Visualize it. Think about it positively, because it could happen."

And that's exactly what happened. Baylor fell behind in the first half of the ball game, 7–0. Then, Auburn was on our one-yard line, first and goal to go. The play was run. Someone hit the Auburn running back head on. The ball squirted out of his hands and into our own end zone. We recovered, getting the football out on the twenty-yard line. We immediately drove the length of the field and tied the score at half time, 7–7. In the second half Auburn went ahead 14–7. In the waning minutes of the football game, we drove the length of the field, scored, went for two points, made them and won the game 15–14. It was a one great comeback for Baylor football. The secret was this: We had already experienced the situation mentally. We expected good things to happen and they did; someone had to make the big play; and someone had to score the winning touchdown and the two points afterward to give Baylor a victory.

The next week we were to play the University of Illinois in Champaign. Illinois was off to its greatest start in many years. It had knocked off Missouri, was ranked nationally and was unde-feated. In the game against Baylor, Illinois received the opening kickoff, drove the length of the field and scored. The Illinois home crowd was enthusiastic and happy, waiting for the total collapse of the Bears from Waco and waiting to add one more game to their win column. But it was not to be. The Bears came from behind and won a convincing victory 34–19 in a televised game.

Lesson taught. Lesson learned. This would prove to be a team of immense character, with great power in its capacity to never give up and never quit.

Some even more interesting dynamics would occur on the road to playing South Carolina the following week. To begin with, there were numerous reasons why it was important to me to beat the South Carolina Gamecocks. First, Jim Carlin, the head football coach at South Carolina, is a good friend of mine, but there's not anybody I'd rather defeat on the football field than Jim and his team. Jim feels the same way about me. Jim Carlin has proven himself to be an outstanding coach and he had a tremendous program going at South Carolina, making the rivalry between us all the more intense. Second, we were now at two and one for the season and a win against South Carolina could spur us on to having an outstanding record for the year. Our coaches and players remembered back to the 1975 season. We were undefeated coming into our game against South Carolina. We felt the loss to South Carolina then had contributed greatly to the demise of a very good football team. I felt, as did many of our players, that a win over South Carolina was extremely important.

I wasn't truly aware of my own personal investment in this game until the practice period on Tuesday before the game that Saturday. On Monday and Tuesday, we devoted the last ten minutes of the practice sessions to contact periods. We would go to the goal line and take our top offensive players and line them up against our scout team defense, portraying the defense of the opponent that we would be playing that week. I would give our offense three plays, then we would get in a huddle and I would tell the players the importance of scoring.

Our tandem offense has a great reputation for getting the ball in the end zone. These players would take three plays and I would be very unhappy if they did not score with all three plays and the team would be very unhappy too. We would repeat that with our number two offensive team versus another scout team. Then, we would take the number one defense, put these players with their backs to the wall on the three-yard line and let the scout team portray the opponent's offense.

It was Baylor versus South Carolina on the goal line. In our practice drill we were trying to keep South Carolina out of the end zone. It was a do-or-die situation. On the first play, the scout team ran a dive into the right side of the line of scrimmage. The nose guard and defensive tackle made the stop for a yard gain. It was second down, two yards to go. I yelled and screamed, "Keep 'em out of the end zone." The scout team came to the line of scrimmage and the defense took its alignment. They ran a dive play to the left, one of South Carolina's favorites. They made another yard gain. This time the linebacker and the nose guard made the stop. I patted them on the back again. The defensive players were by that time yelling and hollering, "Keep them out of the end zone. Keep them out of the end zone." The offense huddled, called the play and went to the line of scrimmage.

The Coach Makes the Tackle

As the defense lined up, I found myself inching closer to the line of scrimmage, coaching cap on backwards, whistle in my mouth, in a linebacker's stance positioned directly behind the nose guard between the two linebackers. The ball was snapped. There was a fake to the left halfback and the ball moved to the offensive left. The defensive tackle took the dive man; the defensive end also came in on the dive man; the linebacker on my side of the line of scrimmage scraped and was in a great position to take the quarterback, but he slipped. The quarterback stepped outside of him forcing the corner back to come in and make the play on the quarterback. Just as he came in, the quarterback pitched to the trailing halfback and all the halfback had to do was turn up the field and step into the end zone for a score for South Carolina.

Well, at that very instant, an impulse hit me that I suppose was left over from my old linebacking days. I decided the runner wouldn't score. I'm sure he must have been greatly surprised when, as he turned to run up the field, he encountered the coach. I tackled him hard. As the halfback's backside hit the ground, the entire team started jumping and yelling and screaming.

I jumped up, blood streaming from my lower lip since the whistle was still in my mouth as I made the hit. It's a wonder that I didn't lose all my teeth! But, the team was too excited to care about my teeth. Jumping up and down all around me, they screamed, "South Carolina will not get in the end zone. We will win. We will win."

I walked off the field with a smile on my face.

The South Carolina Gamecocks didn't have any idea what kind of an evening they were in for when they took the field against Baylor University on that beautiful September night. At first, I'm sure they felt they had an easy victory on their hands. The Gamecocks took the opening kickoff and methodically marched it down the field, taking up ten minutes and finally scoring. We struck back by taking the ensuing kickoff and marching for a first down. Then, a pitch was made; there was a bobble of the ball and South Carolina recovered and in short order put it in the end zone for a stunning 14–0 lead.

When the first quarter ended, the Baylor Bears had controlled the ball for only six plays. We started moving the ball, but weren't able to score. Fortunately our defense held from then on, and the score at halftime stayed at 14–0.

Equally fired up after the half, South Carolina moved for a field goal early in the third quarter and made it 17–0. But once again, the Bears didn't give up because they had in mind a different kind of finish. They played for good field position and waited for the appropriate opportunity.

Suddenly, with twelve minutes to go on the clock, we scored. We elected to go for two points because we knew that somewhere down the line, a field goal and another touchdown with an extra point would win—if we could make eight points out of six right now. Mark Jackson, our quarterback, sprinted out and ran into the end zone for the two-point play. The score was 17–8 but the clock was ticking off rapidly. The defense had to hold, to do whatever it had to do to get the football back.

Fortunately, the Baylor Bears did not allow South Carolina another first down for the remainder of the game. Time and again, South Carolina was forced to punt. On one punt return, Baylor drove and kicked a field goal, bringing the score to 17–11. With only seconds left, Baylor held again and forced South Carolina to punt. We drove the length of the field to score and kicked the extra point with 45 seconds left on the clock, winning by a score of 18–17.

Baylor's performance against South Carolina reminded me of a quote from James J. Corbitt, the great heavyweight champion of years gone by, who revealed his inner thoughts about never giving up in these verses:

Fight one more round
When your feet are so tired that they have to
Shuffle back to the center of the ring
To fight one more round.

When your arms are so tired that you can
Hardly let your hands come in to the guard.
Fight one more round.

When your nose is bleeding and your eyes are black
And you are so tired you wish your opponent would crack

You know that one more on the jaw will put you to sleep.
Fight one more round.

Remember that the man who always fights one more round
Is never whipped.

The "Psychological Spiral" Theory

Throughout the years, I have come to believe in what I call
a "psychological spiral" in the game of football. It is also applica-
ble to all of life. For instance, in the 1976 season, as we came
from behind on several occasions and won so many football
games, it became obvious to me that the players began to believe
that some way, somehow, in the fourth quarter they were going
to win. No matter what the disadvantage might be; no matter
if they were behind in the game; no matter if someone was injured—some way, somehow they were going to get the job done.

This attitude developed in part because success builds success.
The players realized that since they had pulled the first game
out of the clutches of defeat, there was nothing to keep them
from doing so again.

This desire to win also had to do with a positive approach
that the team had developed toward winning. Our players knew
that if they *thought* success, they would *be* successful. It was
just that simple.

I've also noticed that the same situation can arise on a football
team when bad things continue to happen, especially in the fourth
quarter. It is that psychological downward spiral. Thank goodness
in 1976 our spiral was up! Game after game we continued to
win in the fourth quarter.

But 1976 had another unusual quirk. We had two open dates,
back to back. This created a problem. When we went into the
open dates, it was already bowl selection time, and we already
had two losses. We came out of the open dates and lost only
one game the rest of the season. That should have put us in a
position to be in a bowl game. Unfortunately it did not, because
of the timing.

Coming out of the open dates, we were to play Arkansas at
home. It was to be Frank Broyles' last year as Arkansas' coach.
It was also to be another of the classic games that Baylor and

Arkansas have played over the years. As the score knotted 7–7, we marched the length of the field with a few seconds left on the clock and kicked a field goal that was wide to the left. The game ended in a 7–7 tie.

The next three weekends we defeated Texas Christian University, Rice University and then took a very impressive victory over the University of Texas. We did not know it at the time, but that was also to be the last football game that Darrell Royal would coach against Baylor University. We held the University of Texas scoreless and kept the University of Texas wishbone to its lowest output since Darrell Royal began using the wishbone.

We concluded the season in Lubbock, where Texas Tech was playing for a tie in the Southwest Conference championship. Our sole motivation was to win the game. There was no chance for a bowl game or a championship. Tech jumped to an early lead, but we continued to fight back as had been our custom all year long. Late in the fourth quarter we missed a field goal that would have put us in a tie with Texas Tech and would have cost Tech the conference co-championship. Nevertheless, I was happy for Texas Tech and Steve Sloan, Tech's young coach.

Still a Great Success

Although we didn't prove those early prognosticators right and didn't receive a bowl bid, I'll never think of that 1976 season as anything but the great success that it was. The team's players proved in every way that winning was learning to fight one more round.

Although I didn't have the honor of coaching a bowl-bound team that year, I was asked to be the head football coach of the West squad in the East-West Shrine game in Palo Alto, California. As a youngster, I had dreamed about playing in the East-West Shrine game. As a college student, that chance never occurred, but now as a football coach, I was asked to be a part of this great game.

Mark Jackson, of our 1976 team, was going to be one of my quarterbacks for the West team. I thought it was a fitting honor for Mark who, as a junior, broke his shoulder and had not been able to be the leader of the team that had won the championship. His comeback year of 1976 was itself a rewarding experience.

Now, for him to have an opportunity to play on national television in the East-West Shrine game among the greatest players in the nation was a just reward. It was Mark Jackson's fine quarterbacking abilities and also the kick return and defensive ability of Baylor's Gary Green, who also played on the West team, that allowed us to have an upset victory over the East squad.

For me, the victory was not the most important part of that 1976 East-West game. More important was making the acquaintance of a young quarterback from the University of California at Berkeley. His name was Joe Roth. Joe was supposed to share the quarterbacking role for the West with Mark Jackson.

On the day the players arrived for practice, I received a phone call from Joe's coach, Mike White. Mike gave me some very disturbing information that he asked me to handle discreetly. Even though Joe Roth had been one of the outstanding quarterbacks in the nation in 1976, he had suffered some physical problems throughout the year. Toward the end of the season, those problems were diagnosed as cancer.

This young man obviously had great courage in the face of this dread disease. He was selected to play in the All-Star game, but Mike White told me he doubted very seriously that Joe would be able to play. I immediately told Mike that I wanted Joe to be a part of the team in any way that he could. I knew it would mean much to Joe to feel needed and a part of our team.

The first time I met Joe Roth I remember saying to myself, "Why, this young man looks just as hale and hearty as any one of the other thirty-three young men on our squad." He was vibrant and full of life and excited about his opportunities in the ball game—and about his future in the pros. I visited with him briefly during that first meeting, but later had a chance to get to know him much better. His faith and courage in the face of what was happening to him was truly inspirational.

As the week of practices progressed, however, Joe's health became precarious and I finally had to halt his participation in the workouts. I kept offering very simple excuses to the sports writers, saying Joe had a sore shoulder. I told the reporters that Joe would possibly be ready for the game. I truly hoped that he could play.

On the day before the East-West Shrine game, Joe came into the dressing room at Stanford Stadium limping slightly because his back was bothering him immensely. The doctors had told him that it was hopeless for him to try to play. His eyes filled with tears because he wanted so desperately to be in the game.

I asked him to be one of the captains and he sat with me on the sidelines, to help me call the plays and to work with Mark Jackson. He accepted the substitute assignment enthusiastically.

Later, I learned that Joe rebounded enough to travel with Coach White to both the Hula Bowl and the Japan Bowl. Miraculously, he was even able to play in both of those games. In fact, he inspired the Japanese so much with his courage in the face of certain death that the Japanese now give the Joe Roth Award to a participant in the Japan Bowl. About a month after he returned from the Japan Bowl, Joe Roth died.

Joe never gave up. He never quit. He was always willing to fight one more round. He was courageous to the very end. That says a lot about him as an athlete and a person.

His life also reminds us that we don't always win the battles that we want to win. Nevertheless, I have great peace about Joe's death because I know that the final victory was his because he had expressed to me personally his deep faith. Joe lost his battle against cancer, but because of his belief in Jesus Christ, he won the ultimate victory.

On the day of Joe's funeral, I picked up a book in my library, thumbed through it and opened it to this poem by an unknown author:

"Don't Quit"

When things go wrong as they sometimes will,
And the road you trudge seems all uphill,
And the funds are low and the debts are high
And you want to smile, but you have to sigh.
When care is pressing you down a bit, rest if you must.
But don't you quit.

Life is queer with its twists and turns,
As everyone of us sometimes learns.
Many a failure turns about,
When he might have won had he stuck it out.
Don't give up though the pace seems slow
You may succeed with another blow.

Success is failure turned inside out.
The silver tint in a cloud of doubt.
You never can tell how close you are.
It may be near when it seems so far.

So stick to the fight when you're hardest hit.
It's when things seem worse
That you must not quit.

That poem says it clearly: Winning is learning to fight one more round.

Years later while reading a book on Joe's life, which was written by his mother, I discovered something that really touched me. After the Japan Bowl, Joe enrolled in the winter quarter at the University of California. One of his classes was Rhetoric 160. One day Joe read a beautiful and inspiring poem to the class. Joe's mother described that event this way, "After he finished reading the poem, not a sound was heard. He went back to his seat—still not a sound—then long and loud applause. Many had tears in their eyes. A student in the class told me later that the class would never forget that poem. They all knew Joe was fighting a losing battle. With that knowledge, the poem had special meaning."

That poem was "Don't Quit."

4

Winning Is . . .
Learning to Make a Commitment

Out in West Texas where I was born, the oldtimers say, "A man's word is his bond." I've always believed that there's a strong correlation between giving one's word and making a personal commitment. The Bible says it's better never to have made a vow than it is to vow and not keep it.

I'm always impressed when I hear the word "committed" used as an adjective in front of a person's name, representing what that person is or is trying to become. For instance, when I hear the words, "That man is committed to the coaching profession," or "That man is a committed Christian," the comment always gets my attention. Statements like these carry with them an aura of strength and determination.

In my own life, I find myself committed to many things: to God, my family, the young people with whom I work, my coaching staff, the university, my profession, my nation. I believe that everyone should be able to define his or her commitments as well. That's why I ask every player involved in our program at Baylor University to write a list of things to which he is committed. It is an eye-opening experience for many of them, because amazingly, some youngsters are not committed to anything.

God has blessed me with the ability to communicate and I go from one end of this nation to the other speaking to every kind of group imaginable. Years ago, when I saw that God was going to use me in this special way, I made a promise to myself. I pledged that wherever I spoke, whoever I spoke to, I would always include in my presentation the importance of man's relationship to God. I do not want to do this in a pious manner nor in a pushy way but in a way that reflects who I am.

Recently, I flew to South Dakota to speak for a fund-raising dinner at a small college. The coach who had issued the invitation met me at the airport and seemed rather nervous. Finally he blurted out the reason for his anxiety. He said, "Coach, there are two or three people on our board who are a little concerned that you might be a little bit heavy in the religious area." I looked at the coach, smiled warmly and said simply, "What you see is what you get." I could have rephrased it by saying, "My commitment does not vary." Despite this coach's concern, everything worked out very well.

I'm sure that through the years some individuals have been turned off by my commitment to do this. But conversely, literally hundreds have written me after my presentations and mentioned that they were glad that a football coach would share his belief at a public forum as I have done.

After seeing how helpful it was to ask the Baylor University athletes to list their personal commitments, I decided to carry this practice a step further. Now, when I conduct my football camps for youngsters ages ten to fifteen, I ask these young boys to list, in writing, their commitments.

To a room full of boys at one such camp, I asked, "Does anyone in here know what it means when someone says he is committed to something?" A little eleven-year-old stood up and answered, "Coach Teaff, commitment is when you believe in something enough that you would give your life for it." Out of the mouths of babes. . . .

A Lesson in Commitment

The 1977 football season was truly a lesson in commitment, from the first of the recruiting period down to the very last game. During this period we saw young athletes time and again, in some very difficult situations, who were forced to ask themselves the question, "Just exactly what am I committed to?" As they gave their answers in word and in deed, some of the answers were heart-warming and wise; others were disappointing; but all affirmed my belief in zeroing in on just exactly what one believes in enough to give one's all for that belief.

Early in January, 1977, I received a telephone call from Richard Jackson, a transplanted Texan who is pastor of North Phoenix Baptist Church in Phoenix, Arizona. Although I receive twenty to thirty calls a year from preachers, friends, business acquaintances and others telling me of a prospect, there was something about Richard's enthusiasm about this candidate that piqued my interest. Richard said that the individual was not only an outstanding athlete but he was a fine young man and had an interest in Baylor University. After double-checking with the boy's high school coach for only about five minutes I became convinced that I needed to go to Phoenix and meet this young man personally. When I called Richard again, he asked me to speak at his church while I was in town. I eagerly accepted.

After arriving in Phoenix and meeting with the young candidate and talking to him about Baylor, I told him I would be speaking that evening at the North Phoenix Baptist Church and hoped that he would come by so that I might say hello to him again.

Mankind Is Three-dimensional

That night I spoke on "The Three-Dimensional Man," and affirmed my belief that man is mental, physical and spiritual. I envision man sitting on a tripod, each leg of the tripod representing one of these three dimensions. It is important to develop all three areas, I told my audience. If we fail to develop in any one of the three areas, the leg can become weakened and cause the entire tripod to topple over. Sometimes it may take years for this to occur, but inevitably it will happen.

I talked about the fact that physical man has no concept of what his ultimate potential is. I mentioned that year after year, records are broken in athletic events. Athletes, on all levels, are bigger and stronger and faster than ever before. The same thing is true of people mentally. I spoke of how the average person uses only about six to thirteen percent of his mental capability.

But the third dimension of man—mankind's spiritual nature— encompasses all of the others. It is, in essence, what human beings are all about, and what separates us from the animals.

One of the main spiritual qualities of man that I discussed is love, and I used the example of John 3:16, "For God so loved the world that he gave his only begotten son that whosoever believeth on him should not perish but have everlasting life." I believe this Bible verse is the absolute epitome of commitment—and it falls right in line with the definition that the eleven-year-old gave at football camp, that commitment is "believing in something enough that you would give your life for it."

Jesus, the Epitome of Commitment

As a youngster, when someone told me that Jesus died for my sins, it only meant that some abstract figure died some incidental death in a far-off land. As I matured, I began to understand the importance of that death. I began to realize that the love which God has for us allowed Him to let His only begotten Son die on the cross to set us free from our sins. I soon wanted to know more about this man Jesus. I wanted to know more about how He died, so I would understand His love and His suffering for us. So, as part of that segment on the "Three Dimensional Man," I tried to paint a word picture about Jesus' final agony.

I used a graphic description of exactly how Jesus died—even describing in detail the cat of nine tails with which He was beaten. A cat of nine tails has a wooden handle, about two feet long. Attached to it are strips of leather, braided and nailed and then wrapped by more leather to secure the handle. On the tips of the long leather straps are metal and sharp pieces of stone or glass and whatever else could be tied on it. The metal was designed so that it would perform like a hook. The person doing the beating would bring the whip across the back or legs of the one being beaten. The metal, rocks and glass would penetrate the skin. Then with a technique devised to inflict pain and suffering and damage to a person's body, the whip was dragged across the individual's body or legs, ripping the flesh.

This was how Jesus was beaten. His flesh was bleeding profusely. He had been verbally abused. Psychologically as well as physically He was under enormous pressure. He was weak from not having eaten in hours. Jesus was not only convicted to die on the cross, but He was forced to carry His own cross through the city streets to the execution. In humiliation, He was led to a place called Golgotha, the hill of the skull, to be crucified with two thieves.

The cross that Jesus carried was actually a cross beam which weighed about 130 pounds. It had a beveled hole in the middle and was designed to eventually fit on a pole sticking out of the ground on top of the crucifixion hill outside the city gates. The top of the pole was beveled so that the center of the cross beam would fit snugly over it. The individual to be crucified was either nailed or tied to the cross beam. In Jesus' case, He was nailed to the cross.

One hundred thirty pounds seems like a lot for anyone to carry, but it was especially heavy for Jesus in His weakened condition. As He started through the streets of Jerusalem carrying His cross beam, He was verbally abused. Some people spat on Him while others shouted curses. Finally, Jesus fell and could not get the cross beam back on His shoulder. Someone from the sideline stepped in and picked up the cross beam and helped Jesus carry it the rest of the way to Golgotha.

I often wonder what went through Jesus' mind as He trudged through the streets of Jerusalem on His way to His death. I wonder what He thought as He reached the city gates and looked out on Golgotha, seeing the three upright poles sticking out of the ground and knowing that in a little while He would be hanging from one of them until dead. The reality of the whole episode had to bear heavily on His mind. The agony He suffered the night before in the Garden of Gethsemane tells us that the psychological impact of the whole event had to be almost unbearable for Him.

Imagine Jesus' Suffering

I asked the audience to imagine what it must have been like for Him as He reached Golgotha. His cross beam would have been laid on the ground and He would have been forced to lie down for His hands to be nailed to the wood. Wide-eyed, He must have seen the man with the wooden mallet preparing to drive the five- or six-inch spikes into His hands. What must He have thought of that man? No doubt He loved him, despite what the man was doing to Him. Archaeologists now believe that the spikes were driven into the wrist area, just above the palms. This is the part of the hand and arm that would best support a man's weight as he hung on a cross.

Jesus watched that man drive those spikes into His body, first one wrist and then the other. He felt the pain as the mallet struck repeatedly to push the spikes through His flesh and into the wooden beam. No doubt it took several men to hoist Jesus and the wooden beam into place on the top of the pole. Once Jesus was suspended on this cross, the executioners completed their work by nailing His feet to the pole as well.

There, in an agony reserved for criminals, our Savior spent His final hours before death descended mercifully over His body. Medical doctors now believe Jesus was crucified in such a way that His respiratory system quickly ceased to function. To be sure that death had come, the Roman soldiers pierced His side and heart cavity with a spear.

The words of Jesus on that cross testify to the unbelievable pain He endured both physically and emotionally. Yet, He sighed, "Father, forgive them for they know not what they do." He was also concerned for His mother, and instructed His disciple John to care for her. He cried out for something to drink and was given a bitter substitute. And as death came, He said, "It is finished."

Those who stood near that cross first thought Jesus meant that His ministry was finished. Instead, Jesus' ministry was only beginning. On the third day He rose from the grave and He lives today and forever as the King of kings and the Lord of lords.

As I completed my description of Jesus' death, I looked out over the congregation at North Phoenix Baptist and saw the young athlete for whom I had made that special trip to Arizona. I had such good vibes about my talk that night and about this young athlete's response earlier in the afternoon, that I felt a sense of confidence about the trip. I felt that Baylor University had a good chance to get this young athlete's talents. I also felt that God had used me in His unique way in a community far, far from the football stadium in Waco, Texas.

Soon I learned that the young man from Phoenix was turning down Baylor University and had decided to attend the University of Oklahoma. I wished him well, but I hoped against hope that through our encounter he had made a new commitment for his life, too. I thought back over our time together and wondered where I might have fallen short. I told myself, as I always try to, that if this young man was supposed to be at Baylor University he would have come.

Learning to Live with Rejection

At one time I became personally attached to each youngster we tried to recruit to come to Baylor University or the other schools where I have coached. I used to take it as a personal affront when someone turned us down. Then, I realized that there are many reasons why young men choose to go to various universities. I realized that most often those decisions have nothing whatsoever to do with me. All we can do is present our program as it is and our philosophy as it is, too. This is what I felt I had done with this athlete from Phoenix. I had presented Baylor University and our athletic program in the most positive way I could. I felt I had to accept the outcome, whatever it might be.

However, as I have learned over and over again, God does not close one door unless He opens a window somewhere else. That's exactly what happened just after the young man from Phoenix rejected us for OU. His decision gave another athlete the opportunity to make a commitment. This was to pay big dividends for him personally and also for Baylor University. Because that young man from Phoenix went to OU, I had one more scholarship available. Bill Lane of my staff began trying to sell me on a young man from Highland Park High School in Dallas. He said, "Grant, he's the greatest young man I've ever come in contact with. He's a leader; he's a worker; and he's a winner." When Bill told me the young man's size and speed and the position he played, I was not very interested. When Bill showed me the film of this young man, I liked what I saw— but I also knew that he was not tall enough, big enough or fast enough to be our quarterback. Nor was this fellow the size or speed to play defensive back. So I really hedged, but Bill persevered. Soon we traveled to Dallas to meet Scott Smith.

When Bill and I arrived in Dallas, we discovered a problem: Arkansas was already trying to recruit Scott and had promised him the quarterback position. I immediately offered Scott a scholarship, and I told him that I would give him the chance to play quarterback. But I had to be honest with him, so I also told him that we had already signed some other young men who were supposedly better quarterbacks than he. I told him that I would give him the chance to prove that he was the best.

On Honoring a Commitment

Despite that warning, Scott committed himself to play for Baylor University. Our quarterback from the past year, Mark Jackson, had graduated in the spring of 1976. Sammy Bickham, the player we had thought would start as quarterback for us in 1977, had elected to play baseball and did not participate in spring practice. Throughout the spring we had used Greg Woods, a freshman from Jackson, Mississippi, in the quarterback position. By fall, Sammy, who had had no workout in the spring, was back and ready to play our season opener with Texas Tech. The Red Raiders, with a mature quarterback, triumphed over us that day in Waco.

On the Monday afterward, when we began our practice, we still had high hopes Sammy could lead us to victory during that season. During that practice, Sammy brought his hand over in a follow-through motion after throwing a pass. As he did, he hit the top of the helmet of left halfback Gary Blair. That action dislocated and jammed Sammy's index finger. He was to be on the injury list for at least a couple of weeks.

It was then that Scott Smith, our young freshman recruit from Dallas, entered the picture. Our next game was against the University of Kentucky, which supposedly was fielding its best team in years. Scott Smith quarterbacked that game and played well. We won, despite the inexperience of our quarterback. An indication of how well Scott did in that game is etched in Kentucky's record that season: Baylor University was the only school to beat Kentucky that year. Scott went on to start for us as a defensive back and his personal commitment to Baylor University and to me in the tough years of 1978–79 was instrumental in our success since then.

The next week we lost to Nebraska on the road. We tried three quarterbacks during the game but no one could really get

it going. Basically, Nebraska overwhelmed us with its strength,
its size and our lack of a proven quarterback.

The week after that we played the University of Houston in
the Astrodome. We started Sammy Bickham, who had recovered
from his injury and had been working well that week. He performed excellently, but we lost the game in the last few seconds
of play.

The next week, as we played Southern Methodist University
in Waco, a series of events began which showed another side
of commitment. It was one of the most disappointing experiences
I have ever had.

The SMU game had hardly begun when Sammy Bickham,
again our starter, was hit hard as he scrambled out of a drop
back pass and ran for fifteen yards. He got up slowly, but went
back into the huddle and continued to play. However, the Baylor
Bears were unable to move the ball with any consistency.

Robert Bledsoe kicked a 39-yard field goal to tie the score at
3 to 3. Our passing game was very poor that day. We completed
only 6—17 attempts with one interception. Fortunately, in the
second half, our running attack controlled the game. But we
couldn't get the ball in the end zone for a touchdown. Bledsoe
was kicking great. Our defense was playing great. Even when
SMU took the lead early in the fourth quarter, I was not concerned. Our team drove to the SMU 37-yard line, stalled, and
Robert Bledsoe kicked a 47-yard field goal. His second of the
day. Now it was time for the defense to shut down the
Mustang offense. That they did. From the sidelines, I could literally see the commitment of our team to win the game. The
clock was running down. Both teams were fighting to win the
game.

The score was 6–6 late in the fourth quarter. The Baylor Bears
were driving toward the south end of the field. We ran an option
play to the left and Sammy ran up the field a ways before he
was tackled. After that, he stood up, shook his leg a little and
then went back into the huddle and ran another play. The people
in the press box were getting excited because we were now in
field-goal range and they sensed that the three points would give
us the game.

Sammy came to the sidelines and I asked how he was. He

said "fine" but suggested that we not run a play where he had to keep the ball. On the third down, I let Sammy pitch the ball to a back and we got the football in position to kick the field goal. Greg Woods then went in to hold for the kick and the score was 9–6 with about three minutes left in the game.

At this point our trainer, Skip Cox, informed me that Sammy had done something to his knee and that he could not go back into the game. I sent Greg Woods into the game and we ran out the clock and won the football game.

As thrilled as I was about winning, I was concerned about Sammy's injury. In the dressing room after the game, the doctor said it looked like Sammy had either stretched or torn the ligaments in his left knee but they would look at it on Monday to determine if it was operable. On Monday I personally took Sammy to our team doctors. They took X-rays which showed a hairline crack on the bottom of the ball of his foot near the second toe. There was also another old break showing, and Sammy explained that he thought it had resulted from an injury in high school. He said he had never had the injury X-rayed and had never missed a game because of it. Sammy said to me, "You know how mentally tough I am." I responded, "I sure do." The doctors determined that they should operate on Sammy's knee. The night before the surgery, I spent over an hour with Sammy and we talked of his bright future and he expressed how anxious he was to rehabilitate his knee. Then he said, "Next spring I am not going to play baseball, so I can be the best quarterback Baylor University has ever had."

After the surgery, Sammy became withdrawn from me and the team. As the days passed, it was obvious that the breach was growing wider. Shortly thereafter, I received a telephone call from Sammy, informing me that at mid-term he would withdraw from Baylor University and enroll in another school. He said he did not want to discuss the reasons. Only later did he come by my office to share his feelings with me about the departure. He asked me to help him get a release so he could play football for another Southwest Conference school. I told him that was not the easiest thing in the world to do, but that I would lobby for him. I did as he requested because I really wanted him to become successful in football, in academics and in life.

Commitment in the Face of Many Woes

My woes with Sammy were not the last of the spate of injuries and problems during the 1977 season. Going into the game against the University of Texas, we were 4–5 for the season. We were anxious to end the year on an upbeat note. But during that game, Greg Woods, our last healthy quarterback, broke and ran with the football and was tackled about ten yards down field. It was no ordinary tackle, and Woods lay motionless on the astroturf. Our hearts seemed to stop for a few moments. Later it was determined that Greg suffered a neck injury, though fortunately there was no injury to his spinal cord. He had to wear a neck brace for several weeks, and, par for the way things were going in the 1977 season, missed the final game against TCU.

This final game was crucial to us. It was important that we end the season on a winning note, even if we did not have a winning season. We defeated TCU 48–9.

Thus ended a season in which we had nineteen starters injured. With a record like that, it took every ounce of commitment we had to keep going. Fortunately, for the 1977 Baylor Bears, winning meant making a commitment and sticking with it—through adversity as well as prosperity.

For Greg Wood, commitment is a vital part of his life. He has committed himself to serving others as a medical doctor. He is an orthopedic surgeon, specializing in athletic injuries.

5

Winning Is . . .
Doing What It Takes to Get the Job Done

The lead paragraph in the 1978 college football guide published by one of the Texas daily newspapers that summer pretty well summed up our lot going into that year of competition. It read, "Since the end of spring practice, Baylor's quarterback has been signing in as Mr. X, unfortunately. Coach Grant Teaff and his assistants will have to wait until after fall drills have begun to see who takes the snap for the Bears."

It is not a comforting feeling to go into the season having no idea who your quarterback is going to be, but that was exactly our situation.

On top of that, the opening schedule was an absolute killer. We would open with Georgia on the road on regional television. Next, we would play Kentucky, also on the road, and then journey to Ohio State. To top all that off, our fourth game was the conference opener and it was against the defending champions, the University of Houston Cougars. Needless to say, we lost these first four ball games by a total of only fourteen points. We missed five field goals that could have won all four contests.

All of this was mixed with a variety of other unfortunate occurrences that season. Cleveland Franklin, possibly one of the top running backs in Baylor's history, was injured early in the season. Our offense had an erratic performance, with interceptions at inopportune times. There were also a couple of questionable calls from referees and several dumb decisions by the head coach himself. With that combination, it's no wonder that our team was beginning to lose faith in itself in a big way!

Expecting Bad Things to Happen

As bad things continued to happen, our players started to look for them. I never thought I'd see the day when that would happen to a team of mine. But I saw something in the SMU game that was an example of the dark side of the psychological nature we all possess. The Baylor Bears jumped out to an enthusiastic early lead over Southern Methodist University, 21–0 at the halftime. We literally controlled the football the whole first half. We moved the ball up and down the field, scored three touchdowns and held SMU scoreless. We really needed to win this ball game to get the psychological boost. In the first half of the SMU game, we played like the Baylor Bears should play.

As the third quarter opened, we received the opening kickoff and drove it the length of the field, finding ourselves on the one-half yard line about to score our twenty-seventh point. We ran a lead option play, faking the ball to a tailback with the quarterback either pitching or running, depending on what the SMU defensive end did. Steve Smith made a fine fake to the tailback, stepped down the line of scrimmage and the defensive end took off hard to the outside. All Steve had to do was fall in the end zone for the touchdown and SMU would never catch up with us.

For some unexplained reason, Steve paused momentarily before going for the goal. The SMU defensive end from the off side of the field came across, extended his hand and knocked the ball from Steve's arms. It fell on the one-foot line and the SMU players pounced on it. I could see that hollow look in the eyes of our players as they came off the field. Something desperate inside me told me that those bad things were starting to happen again. And when our defensive players went onto the field, you could see that same hollow look in their eyes, too.

Time after time in the next few minutes, the SMU quarterback completed a third down pass or a fourth down pass to keep the drive alive. Soon SMU was in our end zone with a score to make it 21–7. We could feel the noose beginning to tighten around our necks. A few minutes later, we turned the football over to the Mustangs again and SMU had an easy setup for its second touchdown, making the score 21–14. The noose tightened a little harder.

When SMU scored its twenty-first point in the fourth quarter, the people in the stands knew that the Baylor Bears were not going to win after all. The players on the field wearing the green and gold knew the same thing and acted like it. Instead of looking for ways to salvage the situation in the fourth quarter, the Bears began to look for ways to get beat. And that's exactly what happened. SMU defeated us 28–21.

I've spent a lot of long nights after losing football games, but I've never spent one as long as that one. I didn't sleep a wink. Our telephone number is listed in the telephone directory so anyone can call our home, and that night many did. I finally got to the point where I just sat by the phone and patiently answered call after call and listened to the terrible things that were being said. Fortunately, my family believed that all these calls were from people telling me to keep my chin up, but that of course was far from what the real conversations said. The sports writers were calling us the best 0 and 5 football team in America. How I hated those words! I would much rather have been the sorriest 5 and 0 football team in America.

Besides the phone calls, the rumors all of a sudden became rampant. About mid-week the Memphis *Press-Scimitar* printed a story saying that Bob Tyler, Mississippi State football coach, would be replacing me at the end of the season. I later found out that this story was planted by a certain person in the Southwest Conference whom I had for years held in high esteem. I certainly lost a little of my respect for him when I found out that he originated that rumor. The anguish and embarrassment a story like that causes a coach and his family is never really truly known by the people who cause it to be printed.

However, it was ironic that Texas A&M, our next opponent, would furnish the next head coach to Mississippi State. After our defeat of Texas A&M the next week, Emory Bellard suffered through some of the same problems that I was experiencing. On Tuesday after our game, Emory resigned as the football coach at A&M. I'm sure our defeat of the Aggies in their own stadium contributed to that decision, but Emory was a loss to Texas

A&M and a loss to the Southwest Conference. An excellent football coach, Emory stayed out of football for a year and then took Bob Tyler's place at Mississippi State.

A Crucial Decision

Before going into the A&M game, I had made a decision concerning a freshman running back whom I had planned to redshirt—Walter Abercrombie. I envisioned Walter as being the finest running back ever to wear a Baylor uniform. He came from a high school that had not had a winning tradition, and he needed experience and maturity, so I decided to redshirt him as a freshman. After losing Greg Hawthorne in the Ohio State game and then Frank Pollard in the Texas Tech game, we were going into the A&M game with only a small running back by the name of Mickey Elam, whose special story appears later in this book. Mickey had been a quarterback in high school, but he was too little to play quarterback in college so he was playing running back for us. Late in the second quarter, I put Walter into the game. I prepared him earlier in the week and told him that there was a chance he would have to play. He lived up to my expectations by making 207 yards and becoming the all-time single game rusher in Baylor University's history. He led us to victory that day over A&M, 24–6.

The next week we also won against Texas Christian University. That gave us two much-needed victories in a row. But it was almost a hollow victory because we knew that even as well as we played in those two games, we were going to have to play much harder for the rest of the season to keep the egg off our faces. The early season losses had taken their toll mentally. Our players believed that they did not have it to give. So from that time on, we went into the psychological downward spiral I have described. Mentally, we did not believe that we could win, and we acted like it on the football field. We lost to Texas Tech, then we lost to the University of Arkansas.

And then came another extremely long day in my life. With two games left after this one, we went to Houston to play the Rice Owls. We looked like a team whose players had already turned in their uniforms for the season. Our bodies were there, but our minds never showed up. The lights were on, but nobody was home. Rice beat us 27–0. It was an embarrassing and disgusting display of college football and not what our program was all about. It was a disgrace to what we stood for as a university and as a football team.

I looked around in the dressing room and was bothered even more by what I saw. I didn't see the tears and the pain of having lost our eighth game of the season. I saw instead a nonchalant, don't-care attitude of "Let's just get the season over and maybe we'll do better next year."

The bus ride back from Houston to Waco was dreadful. It reminded me of another arduous bus ride back in 1973, when we had also lost to the Rice Owls. Suddenly, however, I was filled with a strange sense of excitement because I remembered back to that 1973 bus ride and the commitment that I had made at that time—to Baylor University and our football program. I knew that the buck stopped with me. Something had to be done and it had to be done right away. If I let this season end the way it was headed now, everything we had worked for would be destroyed. All of the untold hours of recruiting would surely go down the drain. Turning it around would not be easy, because our last game of the season was going to be against the University of Texas, ninth-ranked in the nation and already invited to the Sun Bowl. All UT had to do was stop by Waco and mop up the crumbling, fumbling Baylor Bears and move on to greater things.

I was determined that would not happen. On Sunday afternoon back in Waco, when the coaches reported to the office to start breaking down the Rice film, I told them, "We will not look at the film nor will we show it to the players. We are going to beat the University of Texas, and we are going to do whatever it takes to get the job done."

I asked the defensive staff to talk about the University of Texas—what they knew about UT and what they believed could be done to stop that football team. I met with the offensive staff, and before they had a chance to say it, I told them that we had to change quarterbacks. We decided that the best way to attack the UT defense was to attack it running. We had become primarily a passing team using the straight drop back pass with no options. "Texas will prepare all week for that kind of approach, but we will foil them," I said.

Time to Change the Defeatist Attitude

The young man we chose to lead us as a quarterback was none other than the little running back, Mickey Elam. Mickey was no more than 5-foot-6 and absolutely could not throw the football, but he had good quick feet. We decided on this approach: to fake a drop back pass, flare both of our halfbacks who would take Texas' outside linebackers out into the flats, turn the two defensive tackles out with our guards, and release the center on the middle linebacker, who would be dropping back into the pass coverage, giving Mickey plenty of running room on the quarterback draw. We would put on a sprint-out pass and run what we referred to as a loaded option for the offensive halfback to the side of the call to block the defensive end. The quarterback would merely keep the football. We limited our offense as far as the sprint outs and the drop backs were concerned. Greg Woods was given the responsibility of running that part of the offense.

The Enemy Is Us

When the players reported that afternoon I moved them all to a large meeting room over our dressing room. They looked as bad as I felt—downcast, dejected, sick and tired. Their body language said, "All that hard work and no results." I locked the doors from the inside, walked in and stood before that team. I told them, "I want you to sit down and get as comfortable as you can because you're not going anywhere for a long time. When you do go somewhere, you're going to go believing that you can beat the University of Texas. I know you don't feel that way now and I don't blame you, but I'm going to tell you something. I'm going to tell you exactly how I feel about you and what you've done, and I expect you to do the exact same thing."

I then told them, "Don't hold anything back. I don't want you harboring any petty little resentments. Where there's negativism, I want it laid out on the table. I know that's going to be hard to do, but you're going to do it or we're going to stay here all night."

I first told them how I felt. "I want to tell you that I am sick and tired of that hang-dog look about you. You expect to lose and I'm sick of seeing it written all over your faces and in your postures and in the way you walk. I want to tell you that some of you guys have disappointed me to no end—not just because you've not played as well as you're capable of playing, but because you've let the negative attitude creep in and literally destroy you as a team. I've been disappointed in the performance of some of you guys that we've depended upon. There are many plays that have been run in the last ten ball games. Had any one of you performed a little better on any play, we would not be in the position we're in today."

I called several names of people I was upset with and said why. Then I said, "OK, now I want you guys to let me know how you feel about me and how you feel about this coaching staff and how you feel about each other."

There was silence in the room for a long time. Finally one of the defensive players stood up and stuck his finger out at one of the offensive players and said, "Hey, I want you to know right now that back there early in the season if you hadn't fumbled down there on the goal line, we would have won that football game and we wouldn't be in the situation we're in now. All you had to do was hold onto that football."

Then the offensive player stood, pointed at the defensive player and said, "Yeah, how many times did you have your back to the wall when all you had to do was make a tackle and stop them for less than two yards? We would have won the game!" Turning to a defensive back, the offensive players yelled, "How many times did you let them throw a pass over your head in the secondary? How many touchdowns did that kind of effort cost us?"

Another stood and mentioned one of the guys whom he'd seen miss a tackle. Another one said, "The punter kicked the ball off the side of his foot." Yet another one stood and said to the field goal kicker, "All you had to do was put it through the uprights and you missed five. It would have made us undefeated if you had done it right." Another player from the back of the room said, "How many interceptions have been thrown?"

Finally, after three hours I said, "That's enough. That's it. It's all been said. It's all out in the open. The negativism. The hurt. It's lying out there in front of us. Now, what we all have to do is accept our part of the responsibility, to turn that finger that's been pointing at someone else and turn it right around and point it at ourselves just as I'm doing." I turned my index finger toward my chest. "Now, turn it and point at yourself and say, 'There is the root to our problems. Someone once said, 'I have seen the enemy and he is us. When that changes, everything else will change too.' Now, you can change if you want to, and I'm going to tell you how."

Thinking Like a Winner

"The first thing you have to do is to start thinking and acting like a winner," I told the players. "You become what you think about. If you think negative, you're going to be negative and it's going to cause negative thoughts. You've got to start looking, acting and thinking like a winner.

"In the morning when you get up, I want you to walk to the mirror, look that image in the eye and say, 'Hey, you are a winner. I believe in you. You're going to win on Saturday and I believe in you. You are a winner.' Now, when you shave your face and comb your hair, I want you to put on the best smelling stuff you have and the best-looking clothes. Get your head held up high and walk across that campus with dignity. Smile at everyone you see. Now, a lot of people are going to walk around you to allow themselves to stay away from you when they see you are a football player. They're not going to say any nice things to you. You may not see a friendly face other than another member of this football team who's in the room tonight. But when you see that other team member, run up to him and grab him by the hand and say, 'You're a winner. I believe in you and you're going to win this Saturday.' Now you do that, and tomorrow afternoon we're going to give you a game plan that I guarantee you will beat the University of Texas, if you'll execute it. You have to act and think and perform like winners. Act like a winner off the football field and act like a winner on it. Now get out of this room. Get a smile on your face and get yourselves some rest tonight because we have a big week ahead of us."

A Change in Outlook

The next afternoon the players reported for their taping and then moved into their meeting rooms. Skip Cox, our trainer, walked up to me after he'd finished taping the squad and said, "Hey, Coach. I'm going to tell you something. There is a change in attitude in these guys. They're acting great today. They really act like they are excited about the game, like they think they're going to win."

That afternoon in the team meetings, our defensive staff informed the squad of the things that we were going to do defensively against the University of Texas. Our defensive players responded well.

When we told our offensive players of our game plan and about the quarterback switch, we told them that it must remain a total secret so that Texas could not know that we were working with another quarterback. There was a stir of excitement in the meeting room. We told them that Mickey Elam would play quarterback in the game.

That afternoon at workout, every player really scrambled hard to learn the blocking assignments and new executions of plays that we were going to use. Our Tuesday workout was absolutely great. On Wednesday afternoon when we finished workouts, I called the squad together and said, "I don't believe I've ever seen a group work any harder and do more of what the coach has asked them to do than you've done this week. You have an excellent attitude. You are thinking and acting like winners. You've got a great game plan offensively and defensively and the kicking game is good, too. You are preparing to execute those plans, but I'm going to tell you that if you're going to beat Texas on Saturday afternoon it's going to take more than a winning attitude and more than executing a perfect plan. It's going to take that extra effort. It's going to take somebody doing the job until it gets done. It's going to take someone making the big plays. It may be distasteful; it may be extremely painful; but somebody is going to have to make the big play. When two teams are equal, the team that wins is the team that makes the most big plays and the fewest mistakes."

A Psychological Shock

When I used the word "distasteful," a story popped into my mind that I had heard former Baylor President Abner V. McCall tell two or three years earlier. I related the story to the players because it seemed fitting at the moment. I told them there were two Eskimos who were fishermen and who lived in the northern region of Alaska. Each day the two fishermen would go out on the frozen lake, cut a hole in the pond, sit on a little stool, bait their hook, drop it into the cold frigid water and fish all day long. This went on for three days. One fisherman caught fish after fish. The other had not caught a one. Finally, after the third day, the fisherman who had not caught anything turned to the fisherman who was making the catches and said, "Here we are within two feet of each other with the same size hole cut in the ice, using the exact same equipment and the exact same bait. Yet you're catching the fish and I'm not. What is the secret to your success?"

The fisherman catching fish turned his head and looked directly in the eyes of the other fisherman and said, "You gotta keep the worms warm."

At those words, his companion noticed that the fisherman's lower lip was protruding. The unsuccessful fisherman knew by the muffled words of his partner where he had kept the worms warm. It goes without saying that a warm wiggly worm in frigid water will catch more fish than a frozen worm.

The players caught the point of the story—that one has to do whatever it takes to get the job done. They also laughed a little at my illustration. Monday after practice I gave the players some instructions that I would follow myself: Avoid listening to television and radio or reading the newspaper. I told them to circle the wagons and build up a shield against all the criticism and comments and to prepare to go on the field and win.

The reason I had asked the players to put up a shield was because on Monday the rumors and the negativism got to me. If ever there was a week in which it was good to have a shield in place, this was it.

The attitude that Baylor University was going to lose to the University of Texas was truly prevalent. Rumors were rampant that I would resign after the Texas game. There were other rumors which said I would fire this coach or that coach or change the entire coaching staff; and that the administration had lost faith in me. All that negativism got to me. About 2 P.M., I called President McCall and his assistant, Dr. Herbert Reynolds, and asked to see them that afternoon. Just as the team arrived for taping and to prepare for practice, I went in for the meeting.

President McCall was very reassuring and told me that he stood behind me in our program. He said it was possible that some changes needed to be made, but said he felt I was capable of figuring out what they were. My trip to the administration office didn't solve any problems but it certainly made me feel a little better—and it certainly made me more resolved to turn this week of negativism into something positive. It was at that moment I applied a principle that I had always used, but somehow had lost sight of.

What Goes in, Comes out

As a child, I learned the importance of a positive attitude, and I discovered that I could control my attitude by the way I thought. As I matured, I discovered that what we put into our minds determines what we think. This is the principle: I liken our brain to a computer-calculator-video recorder which gives us information based on what we put in. Like those man-made machines, what we put into our own brains determines what comes out of them. The way we approach life is the essence of our attitude. If we want a positive attitude, we should put positive things into our minds. If we don't care about our attitude, then we can allow negatives to enter our thinking. Human nature is negative. What we see on television is often negative. Some of what we read in the newspaper is negative. Therefore, we have to put up a shield against negativism and make a conscious effort to fill ourselves with positives. Who we associate with, what type of music we listen to, what we read, what we see or watch, all help determine our attitude.

I've had young people say, "Coach, I can handle smut, pornography—it won't affect me." My answer, "Oh yes, it will. What goes in, comes out."

The week progressed. I felt better and better about our game plan. It was obvious in the players' conduct in the training room and on the field that they had started to think and act like winners. It became obvious that they really believed in the game plan and came to believe that they actually were going to defeat Texas. In Thursday's practice there was as much enthusiasm about Saturday's game as any I had seen since I had been at Baylor.

But on Friday night, as I sat watching a movie with the players, I began to realize that something had started troubling them in

the past day or so. I suddenly realized what was wrong. It had
to do with being able to hold onto what you have in terms of
positive attitudes. I was concerned that all of the bad things
that had happened to us might manifest themselves the first time
we turned the ball over, threw an interception or Texas made
a touchdown.

The psychological downward spiral that we were in had not
gone away; we had simply diverted it and were trying to overcome
it with a positive mental attitude. What the team needed to do
was to just go out, turn loose and play football like these individuals were capable of playing. I found myself wishing there was
some way in which their minds could be freed up from all their
cares and worries. The current 2–8 season in which we were
involved, the game with the University of Texas and the end
of season pressures on this team were unbearable. I sensed it.

Suddenly a plan came to my mind as to how I might loosen
them up before the ball game. The plan seemed perfect, but I
was a little concerned about the reaction the team would have
to what I was going to do. So, during our Friday night movie,
I asked Keith Jones, a five-year senior, to come outside the meeting room. He was a person who really knew the team well and
was also a person I could trust. I told him how concerned I
was about the team being uptight and disintegrating the first
time something bad happened on Saturday against UT. Then I
told him the little plan that had come to me. As I whispered it
to him, his eyes widened, a smile creased his face and he said,
"That's fantastic, Coach. That's just fantastic." I thanked him
for affirming me and asked him to keep my plan a secret.

On Saturday morning at our team devotional, I reiterated the
fact that the team had started to think like winners in its conduct
and in its performance on the practice field. The players had
put together a game plan and were ready to execute that plan
which would, without a question, defeat the University of Texas.
I told them that I fully believed they knew what was necessary
to get the job done. Then, just to make sure it was fresh in
their minds, I briefly retold the story of the two Alaskan fishermen. I dismissed them to go to offensive and defensive meetings
and to tape. Then, I left.

I breezed out to my car and drove down Valley Mills Drive
in front of the stadium. I stopped in two little grocery stores

and people, unfortunately, recognized me in both places. When I asked if the store carried great big fishing worms, I received puzzled looks. As I walked out to get in my car, I looked over my shoulder and saw the people in each store huddled in conversation. I was sure they were saying, "Poor old Coach Teaff. He has lost his mind and is about to go fishing right before the big ball game."

I tried two other places but to no avail. I took off and drove out toward Lake Waco and stopped at a little store on the highway. I walked in and asked the same question. This time I received an affirmative answer. The clerk reached behind the counter and handed me a box. I opened the lid, looked inside and found it filled with big, juicy night crawlers, each about six inches long and all about the thickness of my little finger. They were perfect! I paid the $1.50 for them, slapped the lid on the box, jumped into my car and headed back to the office. When I arrived there, I reached down and selected the biggest, longest, juiciest one I could find. I pressed him into my left hand, ran into my office, slipped into the bathroom, shut the door and turned on the faucet to give my little friend a bath. That was probably one of the first shampoos a worm ever had. I then found a little plastic container in the training room, popped open the lid and dropped him gently inside, with the lid back in place.

I hurried down to the dressing room just as it was time for the players to go onto the field. We went out for our warm up. I walked down to the center of the field and spoke briefly to Fred Akers, the head football coach at the University of Texas. We exchanged a few pleasantries, and I headed back toward the north end of the field to watch our field goal kickers. I reached my hand into my right pocket carefully, pulled the plastic container out, popped the lid and looked inside, all the while shielding its contents from the thousands of spectators already gathered in the stadium.

I was chagrined to see that my little friend was dead, having suffocated in the airtight container on a warm November afternoon. I didn't have time to go back to the car to get another worm and give him a shampoo too. I decided to put my plan to work, even with a dead worm.

Soon it was time for the teams to leave the field, go down the tunnels on the east side of the stadium and into their respective dressing rooms for last minute reviews. I spent the first five minutes with the offensive team, the second five minutes with the defense and then called them all together in the offensive meeting room. We had our customary pre-game prayer, then I reviewed the kicking team both offensively and defensively and covered two or three other details that were important to our game plan. I wanted our players to leave the dressing room and go immediately to that football field ready to play.

Keeping a Real Worm Warm

Three minutes to go before the game, I stepped on the bench behind me in the east side of the dressing room and motioned for the players to come closer. In my left hand, I cradled my little friend, as the players looked up at me.

"I've never been associated with a team that has had a better week of preparation," I said. "Sunday evening you started thinking and acting like winners. Monday afternoon, you began to put into effect a game plan that will win against Texas today because you are going to execute it the way it has to be executed. You've come to the understanding that it takes more than just preparation to win. It takes someone giving the extra effort to get the job done.

"Now, there are those of you in this room today who are going to make the big play, intercept the pass, recover the fumble, make the key block, fight your way into the end zone. You're going to do it. It's your ball game once you take the field and there's not a thing any coach can do for you. But, I want you all to know, even though I can't get on the football field with you, I can perform.

"I want you to know that while you're out there playing and wiping out Texas, I'll keep the worms warm."

I opened my left hand, reached into it with my right, pulled my friend up and jiggled him. I wanted him to at least appear to be alive. I cocked my head back, opened my lower jaw and dropped him into my mouth, letting him hang over the right corner of my jaw. I chomped him about four times, all the while looking down into the eyes of Gary Don Johnson, our big nose-guard. Gary's eyes seemed to glaze over. I then pointed toward the field, indicating it was time to exit.

Joe Broeker, one of our assistant coaches, was standing outside the door. He later told me that he'd never seen a group looser, happier and more eager to play than was the group that left that dressing room.

The players immediately began playing wild. Mickey Elam shocked the Texas Longhorns with his running, and we scored 38 points. We beat the University of Texas by the largest score that Baylor University has ever won by. And behind me on the bench all during the game I could hear the players mumbling, "Did you see Coach Teaff? He put that worm into his mouth!"

Later that worm incident, as it would be referred to by everyone nationally, received quite a bit of attention. It was thought to be a motivational trick that I'd used to stir our team up to beat the University of Texas. It was greatly misunderstood. It had nothing to do with motivation. It was simply a psychological device to allow the players to relax, turn loose and play the way they had prepared and not to be uptight about the University of Texas. It was certainly great to see our disappointing 1978 season ending on a high note. It was wonderful to see those football players who had suffered so much really feel good about themselves.

I left the dressing room to do a radio interview. The announcer had talked to one of the players and obviously had been told that something occurred before the ball game. In the announcer's mind, he assumed I had told the players that I was going to quit coaching and retire at the end of the game. That's what he thought fired them up. So at the conclusion of our interview he asked me, "Coach Teaff, can you share with the radio audience what happened in the dressing room before the game? One of the players said it had a lot to do with the victory."

I gave the announcer a rather stunned look and said, "No, I don't have anything to say about what happened in the dressing room." But a lot of people in the radio audience also assumed, as the announcer had, that I had told the team something startling, like it was my last game, because the local newspaper was flooded with calls demanding to know if I planned to be back at Baylor in 1979.

By the time I got home that night, the phone was ringing off the hook, with people asking me that same question. United Press International called, reporting Mike Singletary had said in his post-game statement, "We were ready to play, but when Coach Teaff swallowed that worm, everybody just went crazy." The UPI reporter asked, "Do you have anything to say about that worm?" I told him, "Look, anything that takes place between me and my football team before the game, during the game or after the game is strictly our business and nobody else's."

He replied, "OK, Coach, but you'll have to understand that we're going to print the story and you may as well go on and give your side of it."

I said I'd cooperate but only if he would run the event in context and listen to the whole story. So I gave it to him—from the beginning on Sunday afternoon until the conclusion with the great victory over the University of Texas. UPI printed the story, word for word. It ran all over the country. Still, the act was misconstrued and misinterpreted by many, even those players who saw it happen.

Nevertheless, I was glad in retrospect that I had pulled the worm incident off so well. It was a reminder to the team as well as to the coach, that winning is doing whatever it takes to get the job done.

6

Winning Is . . .
Not Running from Problems

At the end of the next week, I was to go to Tulsa, Oklahoma, to speak to an enormous football banquet for all the high school teams in the Tulsa area. It was a golden opportunity to talk to a gathering of young people and to help them think about their goals and commitments. I was really looking forward to this engagement.

The day before I was to fly there for the talk, I received a telephone call from a man in Oklahoma whom I had known for many years. He told me that my plans for the trip were about to change slightly. Instead of flying commercially, he told me I would be picked up in a private jet and flown to Tulsa. He added that there would be someone on the plane who would talk to me and that all I had to do was listen.

Furthermore, he said that when I arrived in Tulsa, I would be driven to the banquet by another person who wanted to talk to me. Again, all I had to do was listen.

"Fine, but what does it pertain to?" I asked finally when he concluded his speech.

"The head football coaching job at Oklahoma State University," he replied.

A few days later, the events occurred just as my caller had promised. The man picking me up in the plane simply said to me that Oklahoma State needed me and that I should listen carefully to everything that people said to me that day. When we arrived in Tulsa, a very nice man picked me up and drove me to the banquet. All the way there, he talked about Oklahoma State, the problems it was experiencing and its losing records. He said he felt deeply that I was the man who could completely turn the image around.

A Good Time for an Offer

I was, of course, very flattered. My ego was not exactly soaring, coming off a 3–8 season. I was also impressed with the sincerity of the two men I had met.

At the banquet I "happened" to sit by a young man who was going to be a quarterback for Oklahoma State's football team the next year. He also happened to serve as a student representative on the football coach selection committee. During the banquet, he talked with me about Oklahoma State and gave me his feelings from a player's point of view. Almost every person I met that night had something good to say about Oklahoma State and the contribution that I could make to the university.

After the banquet was over, we flew to Stillwater, the site of Oklahoma State University, where we dropped off the quarterback and then flew back to Waco. The conversation was the same, and I simply did what I had done all day. I listened.

When I arrived home that night, I told my wife, Donell, about my experience and how kind and warm and really caring the people were about their university. That really touched me and made me want to try to help them in some way.

Their conversations made me feel good and made me feel wanted—a feeling that I'll have to admit I had not felt in some time.

Early the next morning I received a telephone call from the man who had driven me from the airport to the banquet. He happened to be a very influential member of the board of trustees and a very important backer of the athletic program. He called to see if I would come visit with the Oklahoma State football coach search committee. He also wanted me to meet the school's president and the athletic director. I told him I would really have to think about it. He promised to call me back the next day.

I hung up the phone and walked directly to the office of Coach Jack Patterson, Baylor's athletic director. I told him of the experience I'd had the night before and that Oklahoma State's search committee wanted me to come up and talk with school officials. I told Jack that I did not feel interested in the job. I asked for his advice about what I should do. He said something that surprised me.

"I think you definitely should go up there and talk to Oklahoma State," Jack told me. "You need the experience of visiting with a selection committee. Someday you may be an athletic director and have to hire coaches. You need to know and understand the process. I think you should go to visit."

I had hoped for a different answer. Since he had given me that response, it prompted another question: What would be done about my contract? I had one year left on a five-year contract. I pointed out to Jack that a coach with a one-year contract has great difficulties when he tries to recruit.

He paused for a moment, looked down at his desk, looked back at me, and shook his head. "I work on a year-to-year contract, and that's the way you should work," he said.

I walked out of his office feeling angry, hurt and sick. I walked directly into my office and called Oklahoma State. I told the people there that I did not have an interest in moving to Stillwater but that I would come and visit with them anyway. I told them my name was not to be placed with the list of those applying for the job, but that I would come and try to assist them in their search. I told them I wanted to help, because I was so impressed with their sincerity and their efforts to do a good job. My contacts in Stillwater asked if I would bring Donell. I said I would. We made arrangements to be picked up the following Monday in Dallas by Oklahoma State representatives.

Before I hung up, however, I warned my contact that I did not want the information about my visit to appear in any newspaper. I did not want word to leak out that I was going to visit Oklahoma State. I told my contact that if I read such a story anywhere, I would deny it emphatically. He told me I could rest assured that it would be kept quiet in Oklahoma.

The next Monday evening Donell and I flew aboard a private plane to Stillwater. We were met there by the athletic director and some very fine people. We checked into a hotel on campus

and started preparing for dinner with the coaching selection committee. During our time of preparation, a close friend of mine
phoned. I had confided in him earlier about the circumstances
of my visit. I had told him that I would return to Stillwater
just to visit and that I had no intention of leaving Baylor.

When the phone rang, the friend on the other end of the line
said, "I think you ought to take the job." I was shocked because
I knew how much he loved Baylor and how much he wanted
me to remain there. To hear him say he thought it best that I
take the Oklahoma State job was terribly painful.

He continued, "I've checked around and I don't believe you're
wanted at Baylor University any more. I don't want to see you
hurt."

At the dinner that night, we had a nice meeting with Oklahoma
State's president, faculty and students who were members of the
committee. They were a really fine group. They made Donell
and me feel just great. The next morning I met privately with
the school's president, who seemed like a terrific guy. I told
him I enjoyed meeting him and I would decide if I was interested
in the job.

By the time we returned to Texas, the newspapers and radio
and TV stations were already reporting that I was going to Oklahoma State. As I suspected would happen, there had been a
leak somewhere in Oklahoma and the rumor spread rapidly. That
night I flew to Carrollton, Texas, for a speaking engagement
and was met by a TV reporter who already had announced that
I was going to Oklahoma State. He wanted me to give my farewell
address on the late night sports news.

By the time I got home that evening, I knew I had to do
something immediately. I was flattered and deeply appreciated
Oklahoma State's interest in me, but I simply could not leave
Baylor University. I had a compelling feeling that, bad as the
situation appeared to be, God wanted me at Baylor and I should
not leave. I called the Oklahoma State athletic director to thank
him for his and the school's interest in me. Then I told him
emphatically not to consider me any further. That afternoon I
called a press conference at Baylor Stadium to announce that I
was not a candidate for the job at Oklahoma State. I said that
my intentions were to coach the Baylor University Bears and
to get on with the business of recruiting.

Coming to Grips with a Problem

Basically, I was beginning to come to grips with the problems of my one-year contract. Once I came to the conclusion that it was no longer my problem—that it was somebody else's problem—I felt more at peace. When I was asked about it in the press conference that afternoon, I tried to give as upbeat an answer as possible. I said, "It's fine with me. The only problem will occur in recruiting, but we'll overcome that."

And that's exactly what we had to do. Later during recruiting, we were close to signing Kent Townsend, whose brother played for me in the early years at Baylor. Kent was heavily recruited. We felt good about Kent coming to Baylor. But about a week before the signing date, Kent called me with a lot of questions and a lot of doubts. Another conference school had been filling him with deep concerns and doubts about my one-year contract. I told Kent that my goals and my plans were to be at Baylor University as long as he would be there. I told him I would do everything in my power to see to it that I was around a long time, and that from my perspective he could count on it. That seemed to satisfy him. I had to repeat that same speech several times over the next few days, but still, we lost some good players. Later when I was offered other jobs, I remembered my promise to Kent.

I've always been an emotional and sensitive person; I've always cared what people said about me and thought about me, but the 1978 season had hardened my outer shell. On the outside at least, I was like a solid rock. I was determined that what I was doing was right and that we were going to be successful at Baylor University despite all the adversity and all of the odds and forces working against us.

So, at my first staff meeting in the spring of 1979 before the opening of spring practice, I carefully explained to the coaches my feelings about what we were going to be doing. As the assistants filed in, I thought about how thankful I was for these men, who were like members of my own family. There was Wade Turner, who had been with me since 1969 when I was at Angelo State; Bill Lane, who played college ball with me and joined me in 1969 as an assistant; Cotton Davidson, who called me the night I got the job at Baylor University and asked to be a part of our program; John O'Hara, probably the number one recruiter that I know anywhere in the country and a person destined for real greatness in the coaching profession; Ron Harms, former head coach of a little school in Colorado, assistant at Texas A&M and a very innovative person on offense; Corky Nelson, who once coached Earl Campbell in Tyler and who is an excellent technician with great intensity; Bill Hicks, who does an excellent job of teaching and recruiting; Bill Mills, who coached the defensive ends in 1978; Joe Broeker, who would coach the defensive ends in 1979; and Skip Cox, our head trainer since 1973. They all sat waiting for me to speak.

The Worth of Each Staff Member

We start each of our major staff meetings with a devotional. I started this one by reading from 1 Corinthians 12, which I felt related well to our situation at Baylor at this particular time. I began to read this passage, which deals with the gifts of the Spirit:

(v. 4) "God gives us many kinds of special abilities, but . . . the Holy Spirit . . . is the source of all of them.

(v. 5) "There are different kinds of services to God, but it is the same Lord we are serving. There are many ways in which God works in our lives, but it is the same God who does the work . . ."

The Holy Spirit displays God's power through each of us: (vv. 8–12) "To one person the Spirit gives the ability to give wise advice; someone else may be especially good at studying and teaching. . . . He gives special faith to another, and to someone else the power to heal the sick. He gives the power for doing miracles to some, and to others the power to prophesy and preach. He gives someone else the power to know whether evil spirits are speaking through those who claim to be giving God's messages—or whether it is really the Spirit of God who is speaking. Still another person is able to speak in languages he never learned; and others, who do not know the language . . . understand what he is saying. . . . Our bodies have many parts, but the many parts make up only one body when they are all put together."

I told the assistant coaches that the next few verses (16–20) could really correlate to our staff situation:

"What would you think if you heard an ear say, 'I am not part of the body because I am only an ear and not an eye'? Would that make it any less a part of the body? Suppose the whole body were an eye—then how would you hear? Or if your whole body were just one big ear, how could you smell anything? . . . But that isn't the way God has made us. He has made many parts for our bodies and put each part where he wants it.

"What a strange thing a body would be if it had only one part. God has made many parts, but still there is only one body."

"Now, what I'm saying is that all of us together are one body as a coaching staff. Each of us makes up a separate and necessary part of it. If everyone on a football team had the same size, speed and skill, it would be a dumb game. What makes the game is the different members of the team using their different skills and abilities.

"I think without question the same thing is true of a coaching staff. Every member of this coaching staff has a function. We can't all be coordinators. We can't all be the head coach. We can't all do the technical detail work. We can't all do Skip's job. Each coach has special talents and abilities that make a contribution to the staff. Every member of this staff is important and needed.

"As we begin this spring practice, my major goal is to come away with the best offense, defense and total staff that we can.

"I have, since day one, selected each of you for your talents, abilities and what I think you can do to make a contribution to this staff. Not everybody on this staff is a great recruiter. Not everybody on this staff is a great technical coach. Not everybody is a great motivator. But everybody can make a great contribution when he is living up to his full potential. Each person does things a little differently. You must live up to your expectations of yourself and my expectations of you."

Clearing the Air

"I want you to be innovative; I want you to be loyal; I want you to be hard-working and get the job done, whatever it takes. I can tell you that when you go through a 3–8 season all kinds of things come up. I've heard a lot of talk about my coaching staff. But I want to tell you this: As long as I am at Baylor University, this coaching staff is going to be mine and the people on it are going to be here because I want them here. But in order to justify my feelings about that, you have to commit yourself to doing the best job that you've ever done. Sometimes it's easy to get a little lax. Sometimes it's easy to let things slide. It's easy to say, 'Old so and so will take care of that. You know, I've been working on this staff for a long time and I think it's time for the young ones to do those jobs that I've been doing.'

"I challenge each of you to find ways to make yourselves the best coach that each of you can be. Believe in yourself. Think that you are the best football coach in America. If I didn't think you were a good coach, you wouldn't be on this staff.

"But the other point is this: coaching is like any other business. We've got to win, and when you don't win, then the negative things occur. I am convinced that we can and will win. Whatever it takes for this program to succeed next fall, we're going to do it. We're going to do it in terms of staff work; we're going to do it in terms of organization, in terms of what we're doing technically, and in terms of how much those players will improve this spring.

"I believe in all of you and you understand that. I have fought for you and I will continue to fight for you. You can look around and there are a lot of places in this old world that may have a little more glitter to them, but I'll guarantee you there's not a better place to coach than Baylor University. We've got a lot of things that maybe are not as good as some other schools, but we've got a lot of things that are a lot better. And when you can do what we did this year in recruiting under the circumstances, then that reflects a lot on this university. You can say that we recruited well because we worked hard, and that's true; but I guarantee you that we had to have a school that students can relate to or they would not have committed to come. I think this school is worth fighting for. I'm a fighter and we're going to fight and we're going to do whatever it takes.

"I'm not looking for carbon copies of me; I'm looking for guys who can get the job done and do it in the right way. And I think we've got that."

That concluded my speech, and as I looked around the room, I thought I could detect a look of peace and release on the faces of the coaches. They had heard the rumors: in order for me to survive at Baylor I would have to drop two or three coaches from the staff. It seems that in football, if adversity strikes, the first thing that happens is that somebody points an accusing finger at an assistant coach. The assistant coaches had understood the circling of the wagons and the back-to-the-wall feeling that I had. I believe they also sensed the determination that we were going to do things my way, but that we were going to do them well.

The session with the assistant coaches cleared the air in an amazing way and made all of us feel better and more committed to the task. I was amazed that spring as I daily confronted problem after problem. It seemed as though the more I encountered, the tougher and stronger I became. Like the runner who runs every day and gets in better shape the more he works out, I felt that I was toughening under pressure. In fact, it began to happen each morning about 6 A.M. When I woke, my eyes would pop open and my first thought would be, "What problem am I to be confronted with today? I wonder if it will be a big one."

7

Winning Is . . .
Sharing a Commitment

As spring training for the 1979 season began to take shape, we had excellent workouts. The 1979 team-to-be had dynamic leadership emerging. The players were determined to rectify the 1978 season. The kind of work they put forth in spring practice was indicative of that.

At the end of spring, our team met and talked about the goals that the players wanted to attain in 1979. I was impressed with their maturity, but I was even more impressed with their determination. No one said, "Hey, let's win the conference championship and go to the Cotton Bowl." But what they did say was, "Let's have a winning season and let's be in a bowl game somewhere and lay a foundation for the future. Our schedule is such that we're going to be playing many Top 10 teams. If we can come out of this season with a record good enough to play in a bowl game, then we're going to be moving in the direction of winning a championship."

Although I was exhilarated by their maturity and their goals, it also occurred to me that over the summer while they were apart and away from their teammates and coaches, that enthusiasm could wane or even be forgotten. That's when I had an idea.

Developing a Plan

I immediately walked to my office and asked my secretary to type up three separate invitations to be posted on the locker room bulletin board. The first was to the next year's sophomores, inviting them for refreshments and fellowship at my house on Monday night. On Tuesday night, the juniors were to come and on Wednesday night, the upcoming seniors were to be there.

Next I went to the training room and asked Skip Cox if he had any helmet striping tape. He gave me a funny look because we have never used helmet tape at Baylor. He said, "I don't think we do, Coach." I asked him if he would mind getting me a roll, in the color gold. The look on his face grew even more quizzical, but he didn't ask any questions. He did as I requested. After he brought the tape to me, I reached into my desk drawer, pulled out a hole punch, rolled off a piece of the tape and started punching little gold dots.

On Monday night, after enjoying the wonderful refreshments that Donell had made, I showed the sophomores some of the video highlights of the Texas game. It was important for them to remember they not only beat Texas, but the Texas victory was symbolic that we could beat any team on our schedule. As we talked, I asked them to slide their chairs closer, or just to come sit on the floor close to me. I told them I wanted to share something important with them.

Secret Society of the Gold Dot

One of the leaders of the sophomore class was seated close to my chair. I reached out and took hold of his arm, and pulled it up close so that the face of his watch was pointing upward and outward so each person in the room could see it. I had between my thumb and index finger one of the gold dots that I had punched earlier. I placed the dot over the numeral 6 on the watch. He looked puzzled as he pulled his arm back.

I reached out and took another player's left arm and repeated the same procedure. When I came to one who wasn't wearing a watch, I said, "Hand me your billfold." I opened his billfold and placed the gold dot on the inside. I followed this procedure until everyone in the room had a gold dot. The players were all so dumbfounded that no one was saying a word. I then said, "Men, you are now officially members of the Secret Society of the Gold Dot. From this night forward, you will forever remain loyal to the society, your lips will be sealed as to its purpose and to the meaning of the gold dot that you carry. But to you as an individual, the dot will always be a special reminder. It is located in an area that you will see daily. From this moment forward, every time you see this gold dot it will remind you that you and your teammates have set special goals for 1979 and you will remember how we will reach those goals."

I also told them to remember the significance of the gold color each time they saw the dot. These dots were gold not only because Baylor University's colors are green and gold but also for another reason. I told the players, "G stands for the goals that you have set. You will be reminded that your goal is to have a winning season and to be in a bowl game. These goals mean that you must, to reach them, work every day this spring and summer toward your own physical development, your mental attitude and your personal goals for the 1979 season. You must think and act like a winner every day in your habits and in your conduct.

"The O stands for the oneness it takes to be successful as a team. You discovered this last year when all around us controversy and negativism were swirling. We put our backs to the wall and created a positive force right in the heart of our team. We clung to our positive attitude and became closer and more successful because of it. Remember the importance of oneness. One of your major team goals was unity. Make it a reality through oneness.

"The L stands for loyalty. Loyalty is a foundation on which to build success. You show me a person who is loyal and I'll show you a motivated person. You show me a person who is loyal to his team, his church, his community and his nation and I'll show you a person who is going to make a significant contribution. Loyalty doesn't mean that you have to agree with everything or everybody. What loyalty means is when a decision is made, whether it be in a meeting room, on the practice field or during a ball game, then that decision is what you are going to commit yourselves to totally. You will see to it that that decision becomes a reality. Being a loyal person means that you stand up for your teammates, your coaches, your school and most importantly for yourself.

"The D stands for determination. Some people might refer to it as desire. That's an important part of success, but I like the word determination better because that signifies that if you as an individual are committed to completing a project, you are going to do whatever it takes to get the job done. Be determined to be in the best condition that you've ever been in when you report for practice. Be determined that you are going to be the strongest you have ever been. Be determined that your outlook will be positive and that you will have a winning attitude.

"One last instruction. You can tell no one the meaning of the gold dot on your watch. The coaches do not know. Other team members, until they have been initiated, should not know the meaning of the gold dot. Let them ask questions. They are going to be curious. People on campus will be curious. This summer when you go home people will be curious. Let their curiosity be yet another reminder to you that you are a member of the Secret Society of the Gold Dot."

By Tuesday night, the juniors were going crazy as to why the sophomores were wearing gold dots on their wrist watches. Tuesday night they found out. By Wednesday, the coaches were going crazy. Those players who were wearing the dots were smiling because they had something that the seniors and assistant coaches did not know about yet. And on Wednesday night, the seniors and assistant coaches were initiated into the Secret Society of the Gold Dot. The rest of the spring the players had a lot of fun, all the while being reminded of the important goals they had set. Students on campus were inquisitive. And so it went, just as predicted.

When the players reported for fall practice in August, they walked into the dressing room. On the wall with a big spotlight shining on it was a beautiful green flag with a gold dot in the center. That flag eventually graced every Baylor dressing room at home and on the road during the 1979 season and every Baylor dressing room since that time. The players began to touch it just for luck, as they left the dressing room to play a game and even just for practice. So, the players continue to be reminded of the goals they have set.

It was wonderful to share our own private little secret, but it was even more wonderful to share a commitment.

Sharing an Even More Important Commitment

I couldn't have made it through those rough days if I had not been sharing my commitment with another person, my wife Donell. Strong, loving and wise, Donell has always seemed to blossom even more fully during a crisis. I could certainly not have made it through some of my years in the coaching profession if it had not been for Donell's support.

Donell has a deep and abiding faith in God. She is a woman of prayer and a woman of great concern for others. Some days she would talk to me very harshly, "Now get your chin up and quit feeling sorry for yourself." On other days, she would sense that I needed her compassion and her understanding and she would hold me and say just the right thing. Waking up in the morning and holding Donell tight and praying together about the day's activities and challenges is a very meaningful part of my life. She has always been so sure that Baylor University is where God wanted me to invest my life. Her strength and her confidence in that has always renewed me and helped me, even in the roughest of times.

A familiar poem has a line that goes, "I'd rather see a sermon than hear one any day. I'd rather one would walk with me than merely show the way." For many years, I've lived with the most beautiful sermon that could ever be preached. Donell's life and her actions serve as a constant inspiration to me. She embodies all that anyone would ever want in a wife: Beautiful on the outside and beautiful on the inside, a great friend, a terrific lover, an outstanding mother in every way, an excellent teacher, a compassionate person toward others, yet a hardnosed can-do-it type person who is very tough physically as well as mentally.

An Episode to Remember

When I think of her physical and mental toughness, I'm reminded of something that happened when we lived in San Angelo. At the time it was a horrifying experience; yet today, in retrospect, it seems impressive and even amusing. It happened in 1970, our second year at Angelo State University. One spring morning I had bounded off to the university to teach a class. Donell had gotten the children off to school and decided she was going to bake a cake. Now, Donell always looks gorgeous when she goes to bed, yet manages to be equally gorgeous when she gets up. She usually wears a beautiful robe, but on this morning while rushing to get the children off to school and racing to get the cake ready to go in the oven, she had remained in her powder blue nightgown. She put the mix in the bowl, and as she leaned forward to push the beaters into the mixer, she somehow hit the switch at the same time she plunged the beaters into the drive shaft. Suddenly, her index finger and two adjoining fingers locked inside the beater blades under tremendous pressure because the motor was still running. By that time her fingers were bleeding badly, and she felt as if she were about to faint. She grabbed the telephone with her free hand, and called my office. Since I was in class she just left word that she had had an accident and asked me to come home as soon as possible.

Fearing she would faint if she continued in that position, Donell grabbed the mixer with her free hand and ran out the back door trying to find someone to help her. She first rang on a neighbor's doorbell, but the neighbor had gone to the grocery store. Then she turned toward the end of the block where a new swimming pool for a complex of houses was under construction. Forgetting that she was wearing a very sheer nightgown, she headed for the construction site thinking she would find help there. As she walked in that direction, the construction foreman drove up in his pickup and said to her curiously, "Are you having a problem, ma'am?" Calmly, Donell explained what had happened and asked the man if he would assist her. Fully aware of Donell's state of dress but trying to concentrate on the injury, the foreman finally emerged from the pickup, went around to the back where his tool chest was attached, found a wire cutter and clipped the wires of the mixer, freeing Donell. She thanked him, put the mixer back under her right arm, held the cut-up beaters in her right hand and went back to the house.

Meanwhile, my secretary had called me out of class and told me there was an emergency, so I headed home. When I arrived, Donell's bleeding had almost stopped but there were several cuts on her fingers that were to require stitches. I was tremendously impressed with her courage and her coolness under fire. Of course, she had sore fingers for a long time.

I have noted since that time that she does two things in the morning before she starts to bake a cake. She puts on her outer robe and she makes sure that the mixer is unplugged before she attaches the beaters.

Donell also has a stubbornness that matches her courage. It's a good mixture. In 1974 we discovered that she had a congenital deformity in her lower back that began causing all sorts of back problems. As a result, she stays in pain most of the time now, but no one would ever know it. Her capacity for endurance is unlimited. The wives of our assistant coaches marvel at Donell's ability to get so much done.

In a typical week, she'll teach her Sunday school class of single adults at First Baptist, Waco, counsel with many of the class members, spend time with our girls, attend church services on Sunday night and work three hours after church on some project of the many organizations with which she works.

The rest of the week is just as busy. Monday she teaches a Bible study. She will cook dinner for Laynes' dorm friends, lunch for my staff, go to the hospital to visit an injured player, watch football practice, take our daughter Layne a care package, make Layne a costume for a program at the university, attend Wednesday night teachers' meeting, entertain the entire coaching staff and their families, have breakfast for fifty members of her Sunday school class, entertain thirty recruits in our home, visit parents of the recruits, then attend a football game on Saturday afternoon and sit in the stands, totally composed and positive. After the game, she usually entertains in our home, and if we happen to lose the game, she has the awesome responsibility of getting me back up off the ground ready to tape my television show by 6 A.M. on Sunday. Then the week begins all over again.

I've always tried to share any success that I've known with my assistant coaches and the people who have been involved in the various projects with me and my family. Certainly Donell, as well as our daughters, have played a tremendous role in any success attained.

A Family That Has Fun Together

In my earlier book, *I Believe,* our family's tradition of playing April Fool jokes on each other over the years is well documented. Since that time, coming up with a new trick each year has gotten tough because the girls are older and fully expecting us to hatch up something annually on April 1. Even though the older two girls now are living away from home, they still expect this.

A few years ago while all the girls were in Waco, we were having a difficult time coming up with an April Fool joke. To make matters worse, Donell had experienced more problems with her back and was in the hospital. As always, I was involved in spring practice. About two days before April 1st, Donell and I had still not come up with a good April Fool joke to play on the girls. I called Donell one evening at the hospital and said, "Honey, have you thought of anything that we could pull on the girls this year?"

She said, "Yes, I think I have something. I've been thinking about this. See how it sounds to you." She reminded me of our scheduled family trip. We were taking the girls on a cruise in the Bahamas. We had saved our money for several years to do this and the girls were extremely excited about this summer adventure. Donell's plan was to call our travel agent and have him write a letter that would arrive on April 1st. The letter would state that there was a mixup in travel arrangements and the girls' reservations for the cruise had been cancelled. It would further state that Donell and I would still be able to make the trip but without the girls.

I said, "Honey, you are an absolute genius. Let's do it."

She called the travel agency and made the arrangements. On the morning of April 1, the mail arrived. That afternoon, Tracy, who was a sophomore in high school, arrived home first. She got the mail, saw the letter from the travel agency, suspected that it might contain a problem needing my attention and opened the letter even though it was addressed to me. Five minutes later the phone rang in my office and Tracy was crying and saying, "Oh Daddy, the travel agency has made a terrible mistake and we're not going to get to go. You and Mother are going to get to go but we're not."

In my most sympathetic voice, I said, "Oh, honey, I'm so sorry about that. I tell you what, Mother and I will write you a card from every port."

I chuckled to myself at how well the joke was working. I decided that I had to be home when our youngest nine-year-old, Layne, arrived. Moments after I walked into the house, Layne raced through the door, full of life and vigor, as is her style.

Immediately, she saw my long, concerned face. I said, "Layne, I have something very serious to talk to you about, but first I want you to read the letter on the table." She walked over to the table, picked up the letter and read it. To my surprise, she then nonchalantly flipped it down, turned and walked right past me over to the TV set, flipped it on and flopped down on the carpet in front of the TV. I was astonished. I said, "Layne, aren't you upset about not getting to go to the Bahamas?" She shrugged, "Oh, Dad, you win some and you lose some, and some get rained out."

About an hour later, we were to leave for the hospital to see Donell. I wanted to get Layne separated from the other girls and find out what was going on inside her head. Her flippant answer had disturbed me. We'd driven about two blocks from the house when I turned to her and said, "Look Layne, I'm concerned about something. I don't understand why you're not upset about not getting to go to the Bahamas."

She gave me a puzzled look and said, "Why, Dad, that's easy. When I walked in and saw your long face and heard you say you wanted to talk to me about something serious, I just knew that it was something terrible about Mother. Then when you said I needed to read the letter, I just knew it was going to be from the doctor with bad news about Mom's condition. When I read the letter and found out all I had lost was a trip to the Bahamas, it had no meaning to me."

Love had set its priorities with Layne, and it's this type of love that nurtures me daily in my home life and gives me strength.

The Support of a Good Marriage

I've often contended that I do not hire coaches; I hire coaches' wives. I certainly would not hire a coach who was not technically sound and who was not capable of doing the job that needed to be done. But there are hundreds of otherwise qualified men who simply are not equipped for the job due to the lack of a partnership at home. In a good marriage, the husband and wife split responsibilities, make joint decisions when needed and work cohesively together for an ultimate goal. In our marriage, Donell and I work together for the ultimate good of our family, our marriage and our profession—the coaching profession which both Donell and I are committed to.

I used to joke and say that Donell and I had an agreement—
I made all the major decisions and she made all the minor ones.
I would decide matters like the fate of the national budget and
when to send troops to a foreign country, and she would decide
the little things like what appliance to buy, what kind of automobile we needed and so forth. That makes a good story, but there
is not an ounce of truth in it because in fact on major matters
the decisions are always made jointly.

There are many areas where I have an expertise and she trusts
my judgment implicitly; the same is true for her. I trust Donell's
judgment on things and I also trust her insight and her intuition.
Many times I have bullheadedly wanted to go ahead with something and she would just say, "I don't feel right about this."
When she says this, I always listen. She has great instincts in
dealing with people. I would never consider hiring anybody she
had not already met. If it is a situation where I must make a
decision immediately without being able to slip away and talk
to her, she will give me an affirmative wink from across the
room, or at least let me know her feelings in some way.

We both feel that as partners in our marriage, we are responsible to each other for our physical appearance, our personal hy-
giene and our mental attitude. We work diligently to build each
other up and to keep our marriage vibrant and alive.

Many times in marriages couples will lose respect for each
other, and their love will dwindle. That has not happened in
our marriage because we both work hard to keep our marriage
together and to help each other become the persons God intends
us to be. We are a very close family and we love to do things
with the girls, but there is also a need to spend time alone together
on our own. Our goal is not only to be good lovers but to be
the very best of friends. This is a great combination and one
that has made our marriage, we believe, successful.

Facing the problems that I have faced and the uncertainty
of the future, I feel that I need a sermon every day. It is most
fortunate that I live with one.

And, through it all, I have learned that to obtain the support
of a faithful and loving spouse as well as a devoted team requires
a winning commitment that is deep, lasting and shared.

8

Winning Is . . .
Living an Abundant Life

In mid-summer I was asked to speak in my home church, First Baptist of Waco, in the absence of our pastor, Peter McLeod; so I sat down at my desk to outline my talk. I started to write and the words began to flow. I found myself being reassured as I poured out my beliefs. I did not realize it as I started to prepare for it, but this one sermon probably helped me more than anything else as I headed into the 1979 season.

My topic was how to have the abundant life. I believe God put us on this earth with all sorts of equipment and opportunities, and He wants us to live life to its fullest. Living life to its fullest includes all of life's experiences—loving, sharing, giving, desiring, feeling, achieving, and so forth. John 10:10 says, "My purpose is to give life in all its fullness." He didn't say, "I am come that you might just live life and go through it nonchalantly every day bouncing off this wall or that." He said, "I am come that you might really have a life that is lived in the most profoundly powerful way that you can live it."

There are certain techniques for doing everything. We teach techniques on the athletic field. We teach techniques in business. There are certain techniques a person must master in order to live life to its fullest.

The first technique is to gain control of one's life and those qualities that one possesses that will allow one to succeed.

Life Is More Than Material Possessions

An abundant life doesn't necessarily mean a life with a lot of material possessions or a lot of education. Let me share a West Texas joke that I believe illustrates this point.

I come from Snyder, Texas—I'm a country boy and proud of it. I'm blessed to have a great job and to know people all over this nation. However, one of my good friends whom I visit when I return to Snyder is living an abundant life, too. He did not go away to college but stayed right there in the area and is doing well. He owns a Texaco service station and is chief of the volunteer fire department in Ira, Texas, about eleven miles southwest of Snyder. The department's "fire truck" is actually a red 1953 Chevrolet pickup. My friend keeps that truck behind his service station. The hand-painted letters "Ira Volunteer Fire Department" are somewhat obscured by the two wooden ladders hanging on the side of the truck, secured with barbwire. My friend runs the fire department with three other volunteers— one who owns a little grocery store, one who has a pool hall and one who has a farm two miles outside Ira.

Several years ago Exxon Corporation had an oil well fire at its field about ten miles southwest of Ira. The superintendent immediately called Houston to get the famous firefighter Red Adair, but he was in Saudi Arabia. So the oilfield workers broadcast on the local radio station their need for help in fighting the fire. They said the first volunteer fire department to get there and put out the fire would receive a bonus. My friend heard the announcement and sounded the fire alarm immediately. The other volunteers all came running. They peeled the tarp off the red pickup, jumped in and took off. In the pickup were two barrels—one filled with water and the other one with sand, and stuffed between the two barrels was a blanket. Out in West Texas, they use blankets to fight grass fires.

My friend had that fire truck floorboarded, going at least 35 or 45 miles an hour. The folks at Exxon had backed up about 200 yards from the fire and were waiting for the first volunteer fire department to get there. Over the horizon they saw a cloud of dust moving toward them, and inside the cloud of dust was a red speck. The red speck turned out to be a '53 Chevy pickup. What the Exxon people saw amazed them; four guys in that truck moving headlong down the hill, neither looking to the right nor to the left. The volunteers obviously had total disregard for their own physical well-being, as they slammed head-on into the fire. The volunteer firemen jumped out—one threw water, one pitched sand and one beat the fire with a blanket. Nobody knows how, but miraculously the fire went out.

The Exxon superintendent walked up to my friend, praised him and thanked him for his help. "I've been to two goat-ropings and a county fair, and I ain't never seen anything like this," he said. "You boys came down that hill headlong into that fire, totally disregarding the danger. What courage!" He reached into his pocket and pulled out a check and handed it to my friend. He said, "Here's a check for $1,500. Now, can you tell me what you will do with this bonus?"

My friend slowly turned and look at the superintendent, and with a pained expression on his face said, "The first thing we're going to do is get the brakes fixed on that pickup!"

This joke reminds us that sometimes in life, when things are out of control, a person can still just run headlong into danger and things will still work out. In this case, these men were successful, but they also could have been killed. They could have burned up their truck, been severely injured or both. They were fortunate. A high percentage of the time the outcome is not going to be positive, when you go into a situation out of control. It worked fine for my friend and his buddies, but I surely wouldn't recommend it.

Gaining Control of Our Lives

In our lives, sometimes we go headlong down the hill and bang into things and we're successful. But people who want to live an abundant life have to get control—finding out what's inside them and what their capabilities are and understanding and developing them. That is the base foundation for living abundantly.

The technique I have found to be most helpful in teaching control is self-evaluation. You have to know what you have or don't have to be able to control it.

Make a list of your assets and your liabilities. I am not talking about finances here. List the qualities you possess that will help you to be successful. Now list your liabilities, those things that hold you back and keep you from being everything you could be. Be honest. Once you realize what you have, then you must accentuate the positive and eliminate the negative.

Develop a Positive Attitude

The second technique for attaining an abundant life is to approach life with a positive attitude. One thing that's wrong with our nation is that we find too many things about which to be negative. We can always think of too many reasons why we can't get the job done instead of one or two reasons why we can.

Though my origins are country, I have a deep love for classical music and poetry. I love to visit Baylor University's Armstrong Browning Library, which houses many of the works of Robert and Elizabeth Barrett Browning. Their talent amazes me, and their words have been very meaningful. When I read their works, I understand the great love they felt for each other and for mankind, in sharing the talents that God had given them.

I especially love these words from Robert Browning's poem *Rabbi Ben Ezra:*

Grow old with me.
The best is yet to be.
The last of life
For which the first was made.
Our times are in His hands,
Who sayeth, "A whole I've planned."
Trust God. See all, nor be afraid.

When Browning said "The best is yet to be," he expressed a positive approach to living. No matter how bad today is, or how good today is, tomorrow is going to be better. Now, I believe that with all my heart, and try to teach it to everyone with whom I come in contact.

In essence, that verse in John 10:10 is also saying, "Live life, and live it abundantly. The best is yet to be."

In teaching a positive approach to life, I have found that training oneself to think positively is essential. The technique is to become aware of negative thoughts and eliminate them.

Each summer we hold the Grant Teaff football camp for young boys. I even use this philosophy on my little campers, sometimes with interesting results. Last year at my first meetings with the campers, I told the youngsters that I was going to teach them how to think positively, and gave them this instruction, "All day tomorrow I want you to consciously eliminate your negative thoughts. The way to do that is to be aware when you have one, so tomorrow I want you to count every negative thought you have. Tomorrow night be ready to give me a report."

The next night I started our meeting asking every boy who had ten or more negative thoughts that day to raise his hand. A high percentage raised their hands. Then I asked if anyone had less than five negative thoughts. Three hands went up. Then I asked if anyone had gone through the day without a negative thought. To my amazement, one hand went up. It was that of ten-year-old J. J. I said, "J. J., you went through the whole day without a negative thought?" Obviously, quite proud, he said, "Yes sir." I told him I was happy for him and asked the group to applaud him.

Later, after the meeting, I felt a tug on my belt. It was J. J. With a puzzled look on his face, J. J. said softly, "What's a negative thought?"

The point should be clear here. Be sure you know what a negative thought is, then work to eliminate it.

Our Times Are in His Hands

The implication in Robert Browning's poem is that God has a plan for the whole of our life, not just a part of it. The apostle Paul says it another way in Romans 12:1–2, "I appeal to you, therefore, brethren, by the mercies of God, to present your bodies as a living sacrifice, holy and acceptable to God, which is your spiritual worship. Do not be conformed to this world, but be transformed by the renewal of your mind, that you may prove what is the will of God, what is good and acceptable and perfect" (RSV).

God has a will and a purpose and a plan for every life. It's important for a person to pray about his goals, work diligently toward them and be tenacious in reaching them. Too many people give up too easily, especially in the athletic profession. Young men come to campus as athletes with lots of grandiose ideas about how great they will be and how many yards they will rush and how many tackles they will make and how they will go on to the pros and make millions of dollars. But these dreams often crumble into a shadowy memory because those who dream them don't have the tenacity to stick with their goals. So tenacity is a third technique toward having an abundant life.

When adversity strikes, when bad things happen, a person who lives the abundant life stays with his goals if they are deep within his heart and planned with God's direction.

Mickey Elam: the Picture of Tenacity

I never think about tenacity without thinking about Mickey Elam, our little quarterback and a committed Christian who has an amazing history of sticking to his goals. I'll never forget the day that one of my assistant coaches, Bill Yung, said to me, "Coach, I found a young man that I'd like to recommend to you. He's a winner. He has excellent speed and he wants to play for Baylor University and he wants to play for Grant Teaff."

I was excited to hear those words, because in recruiting, finding a young man who really wants to come to your school or play for you personally is a really important moment. Bill told me more about Mickey Elam: he had a 4.0 grade point average in high school and was outstanding in every way.

"How big is he?" I asked after a few more lines of praise.

"He's 5-foot-6 and weighs 150 pounds," Bill replied.

I was astounded. "He wants to play quarterback for Baylor University against the people we have to play in the next few years—Georgia, Kentucky, Michigan, Ohio State and you name it?"

Bill nodded affirmatively. I was flabbergasted.

I told him I'd give Mickey a scholarship if he would play defensive back but I could never give a quarterback scholarship to a man the size he had just described. When Bill forwarded this message to Mickey Elam, Mickey continued to hold out for playing quarterback.

Two weeks later on a recruiting weekend, we got a call from Mickey Elam who had gone to visit Texas Tech. He had excused himself from the coaches' office and walked to a pay phone, calling me to see if I had changed my mind. I said, "I would not two weeks ago and I will not today. Only if you want to play defense will I take you."

Mickey accepted a scholarship to Texas Tech, but a desire continued to burn inside him to stay with his goal of playing football for Baylor University. In the middle of the year at Texas Tech, he dropped out, gaining a scholarship release and then getting a release from the Southwest Conference. This requires a "yes" vote from all nine members and is almost impossible to obtain. He then went to work for a full year to earn some money.

The following August, he walked into my office, and I recognized him immediately. I thought he was passing through town going back to Lubbock. When I asked him where he was heading, he said, "I'm heading here. I want to play football for you and Baylor University." I was astounded to learn that he had already obtained the necessary release forms.

Nevertheless, I told him, "I didn't give you a scholarship when you got out of high school and I'm not going to give you one now." I knew his father had died when Mickey was quite young and affording Baylor's tuition without financial assistance would be difficult.

"Coach, I've worked for a whole year and I have the money," he responded. "All I'd like to know is, would you give me a chance to be a part of this program, to play for Baylor University and to play for you?"

What could I say to this turn of events? I told him I'd be happy to give him a chance.

All that fall, I was impressed with how hard Mickey worked as a scout team man. Academically he rose to be one of our top scholar athletes, and when spring training came I granted his request to participate as a quarterback. He did not throw the ball very well. He was not very tall, so he could not do some of the things we wanted him to do. He was a fourth team quarterback. It was not possible for me to give him a scholarship as a quarterback, so I told him that I would move him to defense and give him a full scholarship. He again thanked me for that offer, but said he was determined to play offense for Baylor University. "If I have to pay my way another year to stay on the offense, I'll do it," he said.

He was driving me up the wall, and at last I gave in. I finally gave him a scholarship on the offensive field.

When we started the 1978 fall season, Mickey Elam was the third team running back—still not very big but quick and strong and smart and very much a young winner. We lost Greg Hawthorne in the third game of the season and we were playing Houston the next week, so I moved Mickey up to the back-up running back position. During the game, one of our running backs was injured so Mickey had to play and he made some eighty yards in the game. He impressed me with his presence on the field and his ability to get the job done.

As we approached the end of the season, when so many bad things had happened to us and especially our loss to Rice, I realized that we had to make some changes. Our next opponent was to be the University of Texas, which was ninth-ranked in the nation. One of the changes we made was to move Mickey from a running back to quarterback. He made history as he led us to that convincing victory, 28–0 at the half and 28–14 at the end of the game.

Mickey was very much responsible for a portion of that victory, and I couldn't help but think about the tenacity of his desire to stay with the things he believed in. I could not deter him; bad things could not deter him; adversity, odds, people telling him it was impossible. Nothing stopped Mickey Elam from achieving the goal he set for himself.

At the end of the 1978 season, I told Mickey Elam how proud I had been of the things he had accomplished at Baylor. Then I asked him a question that I had been wanting to ask for some time. "Mickey, why did you stick to your guns on coming to Baylor and playing offense? It would have been much simpler for you to give in and do what I wanted you to do." Without hesitation, Mickey said, "I was convinced that it was God's plan for me to come to Baylor and to play quarterback for you."

Even now as Mickey goes through life, those traits of endurance are helping to sustain him. Mickey learned early to live the abundant life by striving and achieving while believing that our times are truly in His hands.

Trust God, See All, Nor Be Afraid

Another key part of Robert Browning's poem is the phrase that says, "Trust God. See all, nor be afraid." You cannot possibly live life abundantly if you're afraid of life. The key to not being afraid of life is trusting God.

Mike Singletary is a great example of the power of faith. Mike found that by trusting God, he was able to set clear goals, believe in himself and believe in others. Mike Singletary is the best defensive player I have ever coached. But Mike didn't start out to be the best at anything.

At the time I came to Baylor in 1972, Mike Singletary was an eighth-grader in a middle school in Houston. He was a frail, sickly child, who had had pneumonia for three consecutive years. But God placed in that child a threefold dream—to develop his body, to play football and to get a college education. God also gave him a desire to have a positive impact on those around him. Faith played a major part in Mike's ability to reach all of his goals and go even further. As a child he came to trust God and to believe God would give him the strength and the wisdom to reach his goals. He knew the road to success would be rocky and rough, but he also knew that accomplishing what he wanted to accomplish would be ever so fulfilling.

Besides his physical problems, Mike had a theological problem to overcome. His father was the pastor of a church whose doctrine did not allow children to participate in organized athletics. In fact, Mike had two older brothers who were big, strong, physically fit young men, but who never participated in sports because of their church's doctrine. Mike's faith gave him the courage to seek permission from his father to participate in football. Robert Browning said when you trust God you don't have to be afraid. Mike was not afraid, nor was his father afraid to give permission for him to participate in athletics.

It would be an inspiring story if I could tell you that Mike became an overnight sensation in football, but the truth was that he had to struggle to gain the strength and the physical stamina to play the game. He was discouraged by many and told that he should not play, but Mike believed that he should. Each year he grew a little stronger and a little better. By the time he was a senior in high school, he was good enough to be All-District and to receive a few scholarship offers.

When I first looked at Mike on film, I was struck by his intensity. When I first met him, I was struck by his sincerity. I knew from that moment forward I wanted to be a part of Mike's life and to help him reach the goals he so desperately wanted to reach.

Mike chose Baylor University because he trusted me and he believed that Baylor was the best place for him to reach his goals. And how he reached his goals! By the time he graduates from Baylor University, Mike will be one of the most honored defensive players who ever played the game. He is emerging into a great leader. Even in this his junior year, he has been selected as a co-captain for our team. He is a legend in Baylor football, and I predict he will have a great pro career. Mike will use the power of faith to achieve great heights as an athlete and as a man.

A person who wants to live life to its fullest and live it abundantly must utilize the power of belief. Jesus said, "All things are possible, if you believe."

Putting a Sermon into Action

As I finished writing my sermon for that church service at First Baptist-Waco, I could hardly wait to share what I had written with the congregation. I knew I had written not only a sermon but a game plan for making the 1979 season a success. I knew I had to gain control and approach the season with a positive attitude, believing that all that had happened was still a part of God's plan, and ultimately, by putting my trust and faith in God, I would, as Robert Browning said, be able to see all and not be afraid.

In late summer the Teaff clan left for its yearly family vacation. All five of us—Donell, Grant, Tammy, Tracy and Layne—were together, heading west in our green van. As Waco became smaller in my rearview mirror, so did the many problems of the last year and a half. I was determined I was not going to think about the upcoming season until I returned from the trip, and most of the time I didn't.

We had a marvelous time singing, eating, viewing the scenery and reading historical markers. We traveled through western Texas, into New Mexico, over to the Grand Canyon in Arizona, then up to Bryce Canyon and Zion National Park in lower Utah. Then it was on to Lake Powell where we were going to do some water skiing and fishing.

From the western side of Utah to the southeast corner, where Lake Powell is located, there is no direct paved highway. Being quite adventuresome, I convinced my traveling companions that we should take a dirt road through 75 miles of wilderness. It would save us over 200 miles of driving and would be extraordinary, I reasoned. The Teaff women all agreed and thought it would be fun—that is, until we came to the sign at the end of the paved highway that read, "Burr Trail is an unpaved, poorly marked road. Travel at your own risk."

Twenty miles further the road seemed to go in two directions, with no marker indicating the road to Lake Powell. I went to the right, and twenty miles further the road became a trail and finally eased its way into the bottom of a dry riverbed. By now the Teaff women were visibly upset. I was beginning to get a little concerned myself. The tension rose after we saw an old overturned van at the bottom of a ravine. Finally, we could go no further. We had to back up for a mile before we could turn around. To keep me from hitting a rock and smashing the oil pan beneath the van as I went in reverse, Donell had to walk beside the van and give me directions. The girls were certain we would never see live human beings again. It was three and one-half hours before we worked our way to Lake Powell and the welcome sight of civilization! We were *so* happy to see this beautiful, tranquil resort!

Tracy is our fisherman, so she and I rented a boat, loaded our tackle and headed out onto the beautiful lake. In the solitude, we talked. Shortly, the subject of the 1979 season came up. I had never discussed my frustration or hurts over the previous season with her. Tracy is very sensitive and knows me very, very well and she had recognized my anxieties. "Dad, I know this year is going to be a great year for Baylor," she said. "I want you to know I have great faith in you and that I love you very much." I turned my head to hide the tears that were welling up in my eyes. That sweet, gentle vote of confidence meant an awful lot to me.

After the stay at Lake Powell, we journeyed north through the mountains of Utah, spending one night on an isolated cattle ranch. Boy, was it cold there! Then through Colorado, down through northern New Mexico and back into Texas. About ten miles outside the city of Waco, I began to feel tight and tense. The season was just around the corner.

One thing I resolved was to keep a log of the 1979 year on my tape recorder. Daily I would record the things that were happening as well as my emotions so that later I could look back and evaluate my true feelings during that time. Perhaps I might learn something to help others cope in similar situations. The day the players were to report, I hit a low point. I said to the recorder: "I've experienced it all emotionally. I've felt abused, betrayed; I've had every negative feeling that a person could have in the last few months. I felt needlessly harassed and as the seconds tick off to the start of the season, I sometimes feel like a person going to his own execution. But I've attempted to face this season in a positive manner—knowing and understanding that my future as a football coach depends on this one year. If we have a good season, I will continue to coach. If we do not, I possibly will not coach any more. I guess the most horrible feeling comes from not knowing where I stand. Just yesterday, Jack Patterson told me that we had a house divided, meaning that the Baylor people were split on me. Boy, did that hurt. One of my goals when I came to Baylor University was to unite the divided house that was here. If I am the cause of the divided house, it hurts deeply. Although logically, this doesn't quite make sense. Just day before yesterday, our promotion director, Catfish Smith, came by and told me our Bear Club members had broken every record for giving already this year and it's just August. In two hours I'll be greeting the varsity football team for the 1979 season. I cannot greet them feeling as I feel now."

At that point, my voice trailed off, and I shut off the tape recorder.

Then I opened my desk drawer, reached in and pulled out a little yellow 3×5 card. I reached over to the Bible on my desk, pulled it toward me and started thumbing through it. There was a verse in the back of my mind that I wanted to find. Donell had shared it with me during the five-game losing streak of 1978. It had really helped me.

Finally, I located 2 Timothy 1:7: "God hath not given us the spirit of fear; but of power, and love, and of a sound mind" (RSV). I copied it on the yellow card. My mind was not sound and it had to be. The answer was in that Scripture verse: God would give me the power that I needed to get the job done. I had the know-how. I just needed the strength and the power. The Bible says it clearly, "Love and of sound mind." I loved

Baylor University. I loved my job. I loved my coaches. I loved
my players. I loved what I was doing and why I was doing it.
I would not be driven from it. I would not give up. I would
fight and I would win because I love and because of the love
of a wonderful family, and because of the love of God. I would
not be deterred and I would gain the strength that I needed to
be successful.

I stuck the card in my pocket and during the next few months
I always had it with me. Probably hundreds of times I pulled
it out and read again those words from 2 Timothy.

When I faced the squad that afternoon, my mind was clear
and I was in total control again. I knew that I would coach
the way I believed in coaching. I knew we would adhere to the
philosophy and principles on which we had built our program.
I knew that I would not press the panic button and yell and
scream and become a basket case before my coaches' and players'
very eyes. There was a peace in my heart and I knew that we
were going to be successful.

What I didn't know was that the problems had just begun.
The trials were still to come, and truly God would sustain me
in every area, but it wasn't going to be easy.

9

Winning Is . . .
Not Giving in to Fear

The first two days of the fall 1979 practice went well. The coaches were extremely enthusiastic. The players were committed to having a great year. Though no one actually verbalized it, I think they sensed that this was a crucial year for our program. They were really fired up and the practices were intense. In fact, the hitting was so intense there were several injuries. We lost our starting center Keith Bishop for the season. Therefore in our final scrimmage, we wanted to keep the contact at a minimum to make sure that we went into the Lamar game as healthy as we could be.

As a staff, we meticulously planned the workout. It was to be under lights in Baylor Stadium. It was to start at the same time that we would go out to warm up for the game the following week against Lamar University. We would use the same warmup procedures that we would use in the ball game and then we would go through an hour's workout against the scout team. At the end of the first hour before we went into our kicking game, we would have a ten-minute period of contact.

At 9 P.M. the buzzer sounded as it did every ten minutes to indicate a time change in workout segments. It was now time for the ten-minute contact period. I was on the south end of the field with the offense. The defense on the north end of the field was working against the scout team as they depicted Lamar's offense.

At about seven or eight minutes into the period, I suddenly heard a sound that seemed to reverberate throughout Baylor Stadium. Startled, I instantly turned my head to look at the north end. It seemed as though everyone on the field stopped and stood motionless as that noise echoed throughout the stands. In addition to those of us on the field, there were maybe 100 or so other people in the stands watching the workout. Not a sound came from any of them. As though watching a motion picture that had stopped in still frames, I saw the movement start up again as a flurry of activity began in an area toward the north end of the field. I immediately started running toward the spot.

As I approached the scene, I could see three male forms lying on the Astroturf almost stacked on top of each other. Doctors and trainers began to swarm about the pile. Kenny Matthews, the man on the bottom of the pile, had been the ball carrier. He was performing as a running back on the defensive scout team, and he obviously had been running hard. He lay motionless because on top of him also lying motionless was Kyle Woods, a young sophomore defensive back from Dallas. And entertwined in Kenny's legs and partially lying on Kyle Woods was Scott Smith, now a sophomore defensive back. Neither Kenny nor Scott moved because some instinct told them that Kyle Woods was badly hurt.

Perhaps it was the sound made by the impact of the tackle that gave them concern. No one knows to this day. But the two men did not immediately work to untangle themselves as players normally do after a pileup.

Instantly, the doctors and trainers were examining Kyle Woods. They brought out a stretcher, taped Kyle's helmet to his shoulder pads to be sure there would be no movement, and then they taped Kyle to the stretcher and carried him to the waiting ambulance.

Minutes beforehand, Kyle Woods had been an aspiring second team defensive back filled with the same goals and dreams of any young Baylor football player: he wanted to be All-Conference, wanted to get a degree and graduate, and wanted to be good enough to get a pro contract.

Now, in a split second, Kyle Woods lay paralyzed on a stretcher, being lifted into an ambulance and speeded to a hospital in Waco.

I suppose it's only natural that after such an incident one looks back and sees how quickly something like this can happen. Kyle Woods was on the field only about three minutes. During that time there were only two offensive plays run by the scout team. It was during the second play that the injury occurred. During that play Kenny Matthews was given the ball on a draw play; he was clogged up inside and he bounced to the outside. Safety Scott Smith recognized immediately that it was not a pass, that it was a draw play. He started to the point of contact as Kenny Matthews came toward the line of scrimmage. Kyle Woods misread the play and let the split receiver get behind him, which is verboten in football. He was up close to the line of scrimmage. As Kenny Matthews bounced to the outside, Scott Smith went in to make the tackle. At the same time, Kyle Woods was coming from the far outside. When he got in close to Kenny Matthews, Kyle dropped his head. At the same instant, Kenny Matthews lowered his head in a butting fashion, and Kenny's and Kyle's helmets clashed.

Kyle Woods' helmet was forced down under Kenny's helmet and against Kenny's chest, torquing Kyle's neck—hence the thunderous, sickening sound that reverberated throughout the stadium. The instant Kyle Woods fell to the Astroturf, he was paralyzed permanently.

The Most Serious Injury of My Coaching Career

A pall fell over Baylor Stadium. The workout, naturally, came to an abrupt end; I called the players together. We knelt in the center of Baylor Stadium—fearful, concerned and praying that the worst would not occur, that Kyle would not be seriously hurt. We prayed desperately that his injury would only amount to a numbness, and that even now, as he was nearing the hospital, he would be regaining his movement.

Every football coach has the horror and fear of some player being injured permanently. At other times in my coaching career, I had seen young men lying motionless on the Astroturf or grass and had held my breath in fright. But in these other cases after a few moments, I would see the players' arms and legs start to move. They would be helped up and away to the sidelines while I was breathing a sigh of relief. But Kyle Woods was not so fortunate. He was lifted up and carried away taped to a stretcher.

By the time I arrived at the hospital, Kyle had already been X-rayed, and the neurosurgeon was waiting for me at the end of a dimly lit hall. Quickly and bluntly the words echoed in my ear. Quadriplegic! Quadriplegic! I went numb all over. My mind was racing. I prayed and I walked and I talked in a haze.

At that very instant I began to hate that which had brought me to this place of respectability and honor and opportunity— the game of football. I began to hate it because it had just taken away from a young man two of the most precious things that any person can possess—mobility and, I thought, the opportunity to live a vibrant and successful life. I walked away to a quiet corner, buried my head in my arms and cried. In that awful moment, I realized that I was the person in charge. I couldn't close out of my mind what had just happened. I couldn't walk away and let someone else worry about it. The buck stopped with me, and at that moment I hated that position of responsibility.

I walked to the end of the hallway and with shaking hands picked up the telephone and dialed Kyle's parents, Anna and Jody Woods, in Dallas. Anna answered the telephone. With quivering voice, I somehow managed to get the words out—Kyle had been seriously injured, things looked very, very bad and they needed to come as quickly as possible to Waco and to the hospital. Anna did not panic but in a calm voice said, "Coach, we'll get someone to take care of the small children. Jody is not home now but we will find him. He's coming in from work, and we'll be there as soon as we can."

I sat down in the hospital lobby, with the cold from the air conditioners making my body shake even more. Over the next several hours as Kyle Woods' parents made their way to Waco, I prayed over and over again that God would give me the words to say and the knowledge to handle the situation. I prayed that my own hurt and guilt would not show.

When Anna and Jody Woods walked into that hospital lobby, my heart began to race. I stood and moved toward them. I immediately told them the seriousness of the situation and related to them what happened. And their response—one of Christian love and care and concern for me—was the beginning of an eternal bond created between us that will never diminish and will never be destroyed. The faith of loving parents and soon, the courage and faith of a young nineteen-year-old, turned what seemed to be the greatest tragedy of my life into one of the greatest triumphs.

There were many tough days ahead. Nevertheless, it is obvious to me now that the Woods, the Teaffs and hundreds of others who loved and appreciated Kyle Woods made that journey together successfully.

A Much-needed Message from the Bible

The next morning, our football team was scheduled to visit Columbus Avenue Baptist Church. Each year we pick a church in the city of Waco where the entire team and coaching staff worships together on the Sunday prior to our opening game. Although our players were desperately worried and sick at heart over what had happened the day before, we thought it best to keep our commitment to the church. I hoped that something said there would lift our spirits.

After having spent a sleepless Saturday night at the hospital with Kyle, I ran home to change clothes, then stopped by the hospital again briefly before church. Kyle was heavily sedated and already had the holes drilled into his skull where the metal tongs were inserted and traction was being placed on his spinal cord, trying to relieve any pressure that might be building up.

I drove from the hospital to Columbus Avenue Baptist Church and arrived about thirty minutes early. Though my personal membership was at First Baptist Church, the pastor at Columbus Avenue, Marshall Edwards, was a close friend of mine and I looked forward to talking to him. However, he was not there when I arrived. The people at the church must have been able to tell from the look on my face that I needed a private place. They invited me into the pastor's office and I just sat down there for a few minutes. I reached into my coat pocket and pulled out the yellow piece of paper and read it. "God does not give us the spirit of fear, but of power, of love, and of sound mind." Then I prayed, "O God, take the fear away from me. I hurt so badly at this time."

When it came time for the worship service to begin, I walked down to the sanctuary. The players had already moved into the pews and looked as hollow-eyed as I did. I'm sure that most of them had not slept the previous night either. I'm sure they spent the long night asking themselves the same questions that I asked myself: Why do such things happen? Is the game of football worth it? Is it worth the chance one takes playing the game? Is it worth it for young men in the prime of their lives, with so much before them, to be put in such vulnerable positions week after week?

Donell had saved me a place in the pew and I eased into the seat beside her. She reached over and held my hand gently but firmly. She could feel it shaking.

The whole service was a fog to me except what Marshall Edwards had to say. It never ceases to amaze me how God prepares and delivers certain individuals to minister to others at specific times of need, and Marshall Edwards was up to the task that morning in a magnificent and powerful way.

Marshall had another sermon planned for that morning, but when he heard about what had happened to Kyle Woods he quickly acted to change his text for that day. He spoke on Romans 8:28, "And we know that all things work together for good to them that love God and who are called according to his purpose." He reassured us that God had not caused this accident to befall Kyle. "I cannot believe God would strike down a fine young athlete just to prove He is God," said Edwards. "Nobody in the whole universe is more broken-hearted about the accident yesterday than is God the Father." He reminded us that Christians are not promised that only good things will happen to them.

Marshall Edwards said that when bad things do happen to God's people that God has a way of helping Christians to use those things to His glory and His honor. "The verse says every person who places his life in God's hands will see God's purpose worked out in his life for good," Edwards said. "If our life is in God's hands, then God is working everything that happens in our life for good. He's taking what's happening to us and using it for good."

During the next week, every moment that I was not on the practice field, I was at the hospital with Kyle. When I was not there, Donell was there helping to relieve Anna who tried to stay as much as she could. Shortly after the accident, as I stood over Kyle and looked down at his face, he opened his eyes and focused on mine, obviously recognizing me. Then a smile spread from ear to ear across his beautiful black face. My facial muscles had practically atrophied. I had not smiled since Saturday. Conversely, every time I saw Kyle Woods he was smiling at me. The question kept recurring in my mind: How can he smile?

After three weeks of this, I could stand it no longer. I walked over to him and said, "Kyle, I've got to ask you a question."

"Yes sir," he replied.

"Why is it that every time I walk into this hospital room and look at you, you are smiling at me? You're lying there paralyzed from the neck down, you're losing weight daily and still you smile at me. Why?"

He looked up at me and said, "Well, first of all, Coach, every time you come in here, you look so sad I figure you need cheering up. And the second thing is, I don't understand why I'm in this situation, but I trust God. Coach, I put my faith in God. I don't believe a word that the doctors have told me about my not ever walking again or ever moving any part of my body except my mouth and my eyes. I don't believe a word of it. I'm excited about the future. I'm excited about what I'm going to do with my life and I'll guarantee you I'm going to do everything in my power to get better.

"And Coach, another thing. I know you feel badly because it happened at Baylor University, and I know you feel badly because it happened in the sport you love. But let me tell you. I don't blame football. I don't blame anybody or anything. It was a situation that just happened. I'm not bitter, nor will I ever be. It's just something that happened and I'm going to make the best of it. You can count on me."

I turned away with tears in my eyes. Here was a nineteen-year-old quadriplegic giving me a great philosophy for life. What courage! What faith! He was an inspiration. Not only did he inspire me, he also inspired his teammates. As they saw his condition and his great spirit, it helped them overcome the grief that they were suffering and the trauma that they had gone through. For the next few weeks, every time someone made a tackle on the field, each player held his breath. We take for granted things like our mobility, and then we see an accident like Kyle's and we realize that in an instant it can all be taken away. The appreciation all of us on the team had for life became boundless.

The Season Begins Despite the Tragedy

While still numb from the shock of Kyle's injury, we won our opening game against Lamar University. The fans weren't too impressed with the score of 20–14, but I was pleased to get the players back on the field in a game. I feel that we won that day by sheer determination and the resolve to fight and not to lose. The team was still suffering greatly from the trauma of losing Kyle.

Our second game was a conference match against one of Baylor University's historic rivals, Texas A&M University. It was essential to win this game if we were going to have a chance at the conference championship and the kind of season that would put us in a bowl game with a winning year. We had to win this game, because the following game was against Alabama on its home turf.

Another Complication Unravels

With my mind lost on thoughts about Kyle and the embryonic season, I was startled to be summoned into the office of our athletic director, Coach Jack Patterson. Quickly and succinctly, he told me a rumor had started that Baylor was under NCAA investigation. He said a local newspaper was going to release the story and that he was about to be interviewed.

I asked immediately, "What investigation?"

He said, "Well, we received a letter from the NCAA inquiring about a young man's second visit to our campus." Under NCAA regulations a youngster can only have one paid visit to any campus. A second visit paid for by a school is illegal.

"Coach Patterson, we've never brought anyone illegally to this campus and never will," I said. "What are you talking about?"

He handed me a copy of the letter. Immediately I recognized the young man and knew the situation. The youngster lived in a community about ten miles outside of Waco. We had brought him in for a paid visit. He was being recruited by another Southwest Conference school. Some of that school's players had tried to encourage him to go to their school. They had picked him up at his home, driven him to a night club in Waco and then brought him by our athletic dormitory. As strange as it might seem, some of the boys from the opposing school knew some of our players and brought the young recruit with them to visit the Baylor University campus. We were not in violation. The other school was in violation, because it is absolutely against the rules and regulations to transport a youngster anywhere for any entertainment, unless he is at your school on his official paid visit.

"Coach Patterson, there is absolutely nothing to this," I said. "Besides, I see from this letter that it is merely a letter of inquiry. I happen to know that the NCAA sends out 150 of these a year when they get information on a possible infraction. They just write the school asking for an explanation of the situation, and I will furnish all the explanation they need concerning this young man's second visit to our campus. I can assure you it will clear us completely."

I went to the practice field almost chuckling about it, because it was obvious that someone had started the rumor hoping there was more to it. I felt the last laugh was on whoever started that rumor.

My surprise, therefore, was immense the next morning when I opened the Tuesday Waco newspaper and saw the headlines announcing that Baylor was under NCAA investigation. The story said Baylor had already been contacted by the NCAA investigator and had also been contacted by the infractions committee of the NCAA. There had been no contact from anyone except a letter of inquiry from the NCAA.

When I arrived at the office that morning, my blood pressure had just about gone out the top. I was madder than the proverbial old wet hen. Once in my office, I started calling our players that I knew had seen the players from the other school with the athlete on our campus. By that afternoon I had four or five of them lined up to make sworn affidavits, which we had notarized. By Thursday afternoon, I had a stack of information a little over an inch thick that I turned over to Coach Patterson and to Judge McCall. The information not only clearly showed we were innocent, but it also seriously incriminated another conference school.

But in the meantime, the story had spread across the state, and I had to spend a good portion of my time answering telephone

calls about the alleged investigation. I repeated my original statement over and over: "We received only a letter of inquiry. We
have sent all of the pertinent information to the NCAA and
that's the last anybody will ever hear of that." And of course
it was the last that anyone heard about it because we were cleared
totally. I'm sad to say no newspaper ever made any type of retrac-
tion. Only Dave Campbell of the *Waco Tribune-Herald* tried
to set the record straight. Nevertheless, I was satisfied that I
had met this challenge headon, handled it intelligently and kept
my control all the while.

The Team Kept Trying

During the following Saturday night's game against Texas
A&M, we played almost flawless football and we walked off the
field with our second victory in two starts. That gave us a good
springboard for the next week's game against a great team from
Tuscaloosa, Alabama—the University of Alabama coached by
Bear Bryant.

I felt our team was honored that night when it played in Birmingham as a sell-out crowd of 79,000 people turned out to
see Baylor and Alabama play. However, Alabama just completely
shut us down offensively. Mike Brannon hurt his thumb before
two-a-day workouts had begun and he could not throw the football. Mickey Elam was a running quarterback and certainly
couldn't throw.

Our defense played an incredible football game. Mike Singletary was all over the football field. It was 14–0 at halftime and
17–0 going into the fourth quarter. Our defense had been on
the field most of the night. One of our linebackers received a
knee injury, putting him out for the rest of the year. I then
made the fateful decision to pull out our top defensive people
who had been in most of the night, put them on the sideline
and take our lumps with younger defensive people. The lumps
were great because we ended up losing 45–0. We did, however,
maintain the health of our defense so the players could fight
another day. The media felt that decision took a lot of courage,
but to us it was the only logical thing to do. We could not win
against Alabama, and to needlessly allow our defensive personnel
to remain on the field and be susceptible to injury did not mesh

with our goals for the rest of the season, especially regarding the Southwest Conference.

The next week we played a very important conference game against Texas Tech University. We played Tech in Waco and felt it was imperative for us to win. As we started the game, we had just come off of having 45 continuous points scored on us without our answering back. As we barely got into the first quarter, Texas Tech added 10 more points to that total. That meant we had gone through 55 points with our offense unable to score.

But we hung in there and in the second quarter got the break that we wanted. We blocked a punt, fell on it in Texas Tech's end zone for a touchdown and kicked the extra point. After that, the momentum of the ball game changed and we went on to win rather easily. Our dressing room after the game was the scene of great excitement. We were now 3–1 on the season; we had emerged from a real good whipping by Alabama into a game that we had to win; we fell behind by 10 points and then did what was necessary to win.

A Strange Twist of Events

Immediately after lunch the next day, I started getting telephone calls from all over the state. They were from alumni and supporters of Baylor University football. They demanded to know why I was on a one-year contract, and asked me to please stay at Baylor University. I couldn't imagine why all of a sudden there was so much ruckus over my one-year contract. Finally I asked one of the callers what the deal was. He said, "You mean you haven't seen the *Dallas Morning News?* Read Mike Jones' article and you will see why we are all so upset." I immediately rushed out and bought a Sunday paper. Mike Jones is one of the most enjoyable writers on the sports scene today. He has a unique way with words and he is widely read. The headlines jumped out at me: "Teaff's critics rest in peace." The article said, "The sound you hear from Waco these days is silence coming from a lot of people who've been doing a lot of talking during the off season. Yes, so the grapevine says, Grant Teaff was given the word—win this season or else. Whether he was called before the board of deacons at Seventh and James Baptist, before old

Abner himself, the man who sits at Abner's right hand, vice-president Reynolds, Athletic Director Jack Patterson or a lynch mob composed of angry Royal Ambassadors, nobody said. The grapevine wasn't party to that information. And you can be sure, under threat of withholding a sweaty quarter from the collection plate, whoever it was that issued such a ridiculous ultimatum has for the moment turned to page 124 in his Broadman Hymnal and is quietly committing to memory the second verse of 'Just as I am.' "

Jones continued, "Still the rumors persist. The same scavengers, some of whom declared Teaff should be given the lifetime contract back in that championship season of 1974, now have been observed casting stones. But after all, what has Teaff done for Baylor besides winning its only championship since the Sermon on the Mount? Nothing. Nothing except bring respectability to a program that was one of the laughing stocks of the country and had its last winning season in 1963. Teaff's first team in 1972 equaled the number of wins of any Baylor team since then. In seven seasons Teaff's teams won more games than had been won in the previous decade. Teaff also has been articulate, readily available and a likeable spokesman both for his school and the Southwest Conference as well as for his faith."

Jones then talked about the Alabama game the previous week and the Oklahoma State situation in 1978. "Nobody came forward bearing such niceties as a new contract after a trying 3–8 season. When the subject of the final year of his contract came up in late summer, Teaff did a remarkable job of retaining his composure, but the usually warm countenance hardened just for an instant. 'I'm sure anyone feels a little pressure when he has one year on his contract,' Teaff said. 'The key is not to let it affect you and force you to coach differently than before. I've seen teams crumble in situations like that. I'm a realist, but I'm determined that I'm going to stick to the principles I believe in.'

"Teaff concluded that portion of the summer conversation with these words, the intent of which seem to be perfectly clear. 'I fully believe that I'll be coaching somewhere next year,' he said."

The last paragraph in Jones' story concluded by saying, "I don't think anyone at Baylor is going to fire Grant Teaff. They just might not get the opportunity, and you can drop that in the collection plate any day of the week."

That last paragraph was probably the match that ignited so many people on that first Monday of October, 1979.

I personally had not made an issue publicly of the one-year contract. But after the Jones article, it seemed that the word on the Baylor grapevine spread rapidly. On Tuesday after the Tech game, I was told that I would be offered a five-year contract. In one sense I was pleased, although I truthfully had overcome the concern and fear that I had felt earlier about it. I had simply decided that the contract business was somebody else's problem; it was certainly not mine.

But when the contract finally came, I experienced a twinge of bitterness. Perhaps I had been hurt more than I realized. The next week, we trounced Army 55–0. Frank Fallon of KWTX radio station in Waco interviewed me from the dressing room at West Point. When he asked me when I would sign the new contract that I'd been offered, I said, "I don't know that I will." Almost immediately I regretted saying that. I suppose I was feeling very exuberant from having won a big game by a big score and knowing that it was now my decision about whether to give Baylor University a new five-year contract or not. I didn't mean to sound cocky; I guess my utter humanity was creeping through at the moment.

However, Baylor Homecoming was the next weekend, and all the trustees and the alumni from across the country would be coming back to campus. The first two days of the week I thought about it seriously. I did not want to be a part of any divisive force that would affect our university, nor did I in any way want to hurt Dr. McCall and Dr. Reynolds, who through the years had been most kind and gracious to me. I was afraid that if I rejected the contract it would in some way reflect on them. I did not want that to happen. So on Thursday before Homecoming I signed the new five-year contract.

LSU Makes a Special Offer

The next morning after signing, I received a telephone call from Paul Dietzel, the athletic director at Louisiana State University, which has always had a prestigious football team. He said he wanted to talk about the vacancy that they would have at that school at the end of the year. I told him that we had an open date the next week after the TCU game, and I asked if I could meet with him then. He insisted that we get together sooner. I had known Paul for many years and respected him both as a coach and now as an athletic director, so I said I would visit with him as soon as possible. The following Monday night I drove into Fort Worth and went to the Holiday Inn south of the Dallas/Fort Worth Airport. Paul was waiting for me there, just as he had said.

The visit had started out as merely an exploratory act on both parts, but mutual feelings soon developed that together we could do some outstanding things with the football program at LSU. I tried to be as honest as I could and I told him that I didn't see how he could consider me for the job. First of all, I didn't have the super record of some of the coaches that he could hire. Secondly, I was being sued by my former player, Sammy Bickham, who had been a quarterback of ours in the ill-fated 1977 season. I explained that I was very hurt by the suit, and that I was puzzled by the deterioration of my personal relationship with Sammy. I found myself telling Coach Dietzel what a fine young man Sammy was. Even with the impending suit, I still felt strongly about Sammy. Paul seemingly recognized my hurt, and said some very encouraging things. Then, to the best of my knowledge I related what I thought had happened. Going over the details of Sammy's injury in the SMU game, and the events that followed, finally I said, "I don't think the suit will ever come to trial," and it never did.

The third reason was Kyle Woods. I felt a special obligation to Kyle that may be difficult for some people to understand. After Kyle's injury, I had immersed myself in raising funds for his rehabilitation. I told Paul Dietzel that a move to another state would seriously jeopardize that fund-raising effort.

Paul wanted to answer my objections one by one. "First of all," he said, "I know what your record is and I know what you have had to overcome to attain that record. Had you been at a state school all the years you have been at Baylor University and had a state school's facilities and backing, your record would have been an outstanding one. As for the suit, don't think another thought about it. These situations always seem to work out, and I have every confidence this problem will not be a problem. And the third thing, wherever you are, you can help Kyle Woods. You can help raise funds for him and you can get the job done in Louisiana as well as in Texas."

He concluded with a vote of confidence in me by saying, "You're the kind of man that I want to be associated with, that I want to have leading our football program. I think you can do a lot for the university and a lot for the state."

As we said good-bye, I reminded him that I had just signed a new five-year contract with Baylor University. I said I was the kind of person who feels very deeply about obligations and contracts.

He told me not to worry about my new Baylor contract. I promised to give him a decision after the Arkansas game. I knew I couldn't spend any time thinking about it until that game was over. He said, "Fair enough" and we parted.

We talked on the telephone a couple of times after that, but he was keeping things very low key. I appreciated that. I didn't want anything in the newspaper and he didn't either. That's why for many years I would not even mention LSU's name when telling this story. Oh yes, once in a while, I saw two or three little newsbriefs speculating that I might go to LSU, but every good coach in the country also had the same speculation printed about him, too, so no one thought anything about it.

The Record Continues to be Good

We went into the Arkansas game with a 6–2 record with only three games left in conference play. If we could beat Arkansas on its home turf, we had a chance to go to the Cotton Bowl.

It was a cold day in Fayetteville. We jumped out to an early lead and were playing magnificently. In fact, we dropped two touchdown passes right in the Arkansas end zone. That would have put the game well on ice by halftime, by at least a score of 28–0. Instead it was 14–0 at halftime.

When Arkansas came out in the second half, it was obvious that Lou Holtz had done a marvelous job in preparing his team. The execution of the team's plan was very well done. We fumbled one in the end zone for an easy touchdown for them. Then on a fourth and one yard situation, Arkansas went for a touchdown instead of trying for the first down. It was a brilliant call and it was complete. Then in the waning moments of the ball game Arkansas threw a long touchdown bomb that beat us.

In the dressing room after the game was over, I hung my head for what seemed like thirty minutes and couldn't stop crying. The game had meant so much, and we played so well. We should have won, but didn't. Boy, did it hurt!

We flew back to Waco and I knew what my answer to LSU was going to be the next morning. I loved Baylor University too much to leave. I thanked Paul Dietzel of LSU for the interest he had shown in me. I told him that I was not interested in the job.

As always, I had sat down with my family to talk about the opportunity. Donell was quite supportive but made sure that I looked at the situation from all sides. Layne's comments really touched me. As a freshman at Richfield High School, she said, "Dad, you have to do the thing that is best for your career, and I want you to know that wherever you go or wherever you coach, I will be at Baylor." There was little doubt about her commitment to Baylor University.

However, that was not the last time I heard from LSU before the job was filled. I was called again and asked if I had changed my mind. I had told my family and all of my assistant coaches about the offer and my decision to reject it. My assistants all thought we should go to Louisiana. The truth is, I simply couldn't make the move. I was committed to Baylor University and its football program. As we discussed earlier, commitment is not something one takes likely.

Now a Bowl Bid

The following week was spent preparing for the game against Rice University. We learned that officials with the Tangerine Bowl, the Peach Bowl and possibly the Fiesta Bowl would be watching our performance in that game. The Peach Bowl and Tangerine Bowl representatives flew to Waco and I really liked both of them. It seemed to me that our best bet was to go to the Peach Bowl, if we were invited. It was to be a nationally televised game on CBS and the money looked good. Now, all we had to do was secure the invitation.

Clemson University had already been invited to the Peach Bowl. The Peach Bowl representative told me to call Danny Ford, the Clemson coach, because Clemson had to approve whoever played in the Peach Bowl. I reached Danny as he and his team were leaving to go to their final season game. I gave him a quick overview of Baylor University and our team. He said immediately that it sounded like a sensational matchup, and he would welcome the opportunity to play the Baylor Bears. That, of course, thrilled me.

That afternoon we handled Rice easily, and after the game we were officially extended the invitation to play Clemson University in the Peach Bowl.

We had accomplished what we set out to do: have a winning season and an invitation to a bowl game.

After the usual postgame interviews, I went to my office, picked up the telephone and called Kyle Woods, who had gone to Dallas to learn to live with his disability. His mother held the phone to his ear while I said, "Kyle, we're going to a bowl game. Are you ready to go with us?" I told him we were playing Clemson University on December 31 in Atlanta, and I wanted him to be there.

"Coach, I'm not ready now, but I will be by then," he said.

I told Kyle that I would make special arrangements for him and his mother and father to fly to Atlanta and stay at the Peach Tree Plaza Hotel.

He said, "Coach, I've never been on an airplane. My mother and dad have never been on an airplane."

"Well, they are taking their first trip on December 30, 1979," I said.

We had one game to go and that was against the University of Texas. We lost the game. On Sunday morning after the Texas game I received one final phone call from Paul Dietzel at LSU. He asked, "Have you changed your mind? Just thought we'd wait until the end of the season to see if you looked at things differently now."

I told him, "I can't thank you enough for what you've done for me. You have made me feel like a person who is really wanted, but I'm going to stay at Baylor. I have a commitment here and I plan to be here. Thank you for your call." I felt at peace about the decision because I was sure that feeling inside of me was of God. Nothing had been written in flaming fire across the sky but I knew what I should do.

We had a great following to the bowl game. Atlanta, Georgia, will probably never be the same after the great Baylor onslaught in 1979 and I know the Peach Tree Plaza Hotel took a long time to get over all the excitement that only Baylor people can stir up. I was personally anxious for the game, but I believe I was even more anxious for Kyle to arrive.

On December 30, the day before the game, we were in a meeting in the Peach Tree Plaza Hotel just about lunch time. We were in a large room with an offensive and defensive meeting at either side. When we finished with those we were just milling around visiting with each other and enjoying the great thrill of being in Atlanta at a bowl game.

Every Eye Was on Kyle Woods

All of a sudden, the double doors in the back of the room swung open. There was a noise and every head in the room turned. There, framed in the archway of the door, in his wheelchair, was Kyle Woods. The last time the players had seen him, he was flat of his back. But here he was, sitting. As every eye was turned on him, he lifted his right hand, placed the V between his index finger and his thumb on a knob on the right side of the wheel chair. He pushed it forward three or four inches. Then he did the same thing with his left hand, pushing that wheel gradually forward. He had no dexterity in his hands and he was using the muscle just behind his shoulder on each arm. He inched the wheelchair forward under his own power.

I've been involved in a lot of exciting moments in the world of athletics, but I've never been in a moment as electrifying as that one was. It was magnificent to see the love and the care and the concern that the football team and the coaching staff had for Kyle Woods. It was incredible to see Kyle's excitement and joy at being reunited with his team.

Early that morning the players had come to me asking if they could do something unusual. They wanted to announce to the entire world that they were going to win the Peach Bowl for Kyle Woods. We were a ten-point underdog to Clemson University. I told the players I felt it would be pretty theatrical to announce such a thing. But they said, "Coach, you don't understand. We want to do something for Kyle. His courage, his determination, his faith and his spirit have motivated us so much and there's not a thing we can do for him except tell the world that we're going to win this game and then go out and win it for him.

"And Coach, there's one other thing," they said. "Each player and each coach would like to wear Kyle's number 23 in the game so that he really is on the field and a part of us."

I thought for only a moment before giving my consent.

That afternoon in the Peach Tree Plaza Hotel the team members told Kyle what they were going to do. Tears streamed down his cheeks as he listened. He was so excited and so thrilled by their gesture. When the meeting was over and the players left the room, I walked over to Kyle and leaned down to his right ear and said, "Kyle, in the morning at the team devotional, I want you to respond to what the team is going to do for you."

He looked up at me and said, "Coach, I'm sorry but I just can't do that."

I said, "Why not?"

He said, "I just can't."

I said, "All I want you to do is just tell them how you feel about what they're going to do for you."

He said, "I'll tell you the truth, Coach. I can't do it, because I'll cry and I can't wipe my tears."

"Kyle," I said, "I'll wipe your tears. You talk."

"Yes, sir," he replied.

The next morning at the team devotional I visited with the team for about five minutes. Kyle was seated to my right in his wheelchair. I immediately turned to Kyle and said, "Kyle, I know you have something to say to this team."

With amazing composure, he thanked them for what they had proposed to do that afternoon—win a game in his name and in his honor. He said, "I know how tough it's been for you guys to get here. I've followed you in the papers and I've listened on the radio and I've hurt with you. I know the hard work in the off-season and how tough it was. I know the heat of the Astroturf in August; I know the trauma you went through when I was hurt. I know what each of you felt for me and the concerns you had, and I appreciate that. I also know the heartbreak of some of the losses you've had this year—losing to outstanding teams like Alabama and Arkansas. I know how badly it hurt you, but you came back and you won and you were invited to the Peach Bowl and I want you to know how proud I am of you."

He hesitated a moment and then went on, "Now I want to tell you guys how I got here. I want you to know that I've been through the same heartache and pain that you've been through. First, when I went to the rehabilitation center in Dallas I couldn't sit up without passing out under extreme pain. Finally as my respiratory system began to function a little bit and the circulatory system, too, I could sit up a little bit at a time. Then they started working me out—three hours in the morning and three hours in the afternoon. I could in no way describe the pain and the other hurts I felt—the psychological impact of not being able to perform even the simplest human tasks, such as going to the bathroom. It's frightening and horrifying, but I want you to know that I've made it to this point and I'm going to make it further. I also want you guys to know how I've made it."

You could literally hear a pin drop in that room as Kyle was talking.

"I couldn't have made it without my faith in God," Kyle said. "I don't understand. I don't know why I'm in the situation that I'm in, but I accept it. I know that God has a purpose and a plan for me and I trust Him for it. In Proverbs it says, Trust in the Lord with all your heart, lean not to your own understanding. Acknowledge Him and He will set your pathway straight. I claim that verse and hope that you will too.

"The second thing that you have to know is what my grandmother taught me. It's been extremely important to me in getting here, and it will also be important in doing the things that I'm going to do the rest of my life. When I was about ten years old, my grandmother was about eighty-seven. Ever since I had known her she had walked on crutches. You could see in her face the terrible pain that she felt. One day she called me to her side, sat me at her knee and said, 'Kyle, I know that you know about my pain, but it's important for you to know how I make it through each day.' I looked into my grandmother's eyes and she gently whispered these words to me, 'I may give out, but I won't ever give up.'" Kyle seemingly looked into every eye in the room and said, "I want you to remember that on the football field, but more importantly, I want you to remember that in the game of life. Our physical bodies are weak but our spirit is strong. Never give up. Never quit. I won't."

Being a ten-point underdog, it was interesting that we fell behind ten points that day in that beautiful stadium in Atlanta.
Clemson University is a team with a great following. The Clemson
people paint tiger paws on their faces with orange paint. There
were tiger paws all the way from Clemson University to Atlanta
and into the stadium. There was a sea of orange in the stands.
In the beginning when we fell behind ten points, Clemson's fans
thought they were going to take Baylor University apart. But
on the field, echoing in our players ears, were the words of Kyle
Woods, and the players would not give up.

The Baylor Bears hung in there, and they did not give up
until they won.

We won on national television. Everybody watching the game
on TV saw Kyle's number 23 on a little terry cloth towel hanging
from each player's belt. Each coach wore one, too. The announc-
ers talked about Kyle, the great love that his team had for him
and the courage that Kyle had shown throughout his whole or-
deal. There was a lot of great news coverage and we got a lot
of great remarks and letters about our victory over Clemson
University. Most of the letters, however, dealt with the courage
and the determination of Kyle Woods. Through the miracle of
national television, Kyle Woods probably touched more people
in that two-hour period than most of us will touch in all our
lifetimes.

That night after the game the Baylor people celebrated all
over Atlanta. You could hardly get up and down the elevators
in our hotel. All the restaurants were brimming with happy,
celebrating Baylor Bears. My mom and dad and Donell's parents,
Don and Dorothy Phillips from Plainview, Texas, were in our
suite of rooms waiting for us when we returned from the game.
I ordered a snack, because I hadn't eaten all day. Everyone sat
in the large living room area of the suite watching the Bluebonnet
Bowl that was on TV that night. Donell and I slipped into the
bedroom, closed the door and embraced for a long time. At that
point, I thanked God for the wonderful year, for the great turnaround that we had had and for the lives of the young men
like Mickey Elam, who truly had proven that the best was yet
to be. And I thanked Him for men like Andrew Mellontree,
Mike Brannon, Mike Singletary, Doak Field and Thomas Brown.
We called every name on the roster until all had been mentioned

and we asked God's special blessing on each one. We thanked God for our coaching staff and the opportunity that we had at Baylor. We thanked God for the courage and the faith of Kyle Woods and his family—and for the experience of unity that we had shared together as families.

As I stood on that mountaintop looking back at the valley of 1978 and the year 1979 and all of the painful things that had happened to us during that span of time, I could only thank God for them. In Romans 5:3–4, the Bible says, "We can rejoice . . . when we run into problems and trials for we know that they are good for us—they help us learn to be patient. And patience develops strength of character in us and helps us trust God more each time we use it until finally our hope and faith are strong and steady." It gives us that inward peace and confidence that it takes under adverse circumstances when all around us life seems to be crumbling. It helps us stick to our plans, our beliefs and our philosophies—and in my case, it helped me coach the way I believe in coaching and then be rewarded with success.

Suddenly, I realized that a crumpled, well-used yellow card was sticking out from my back pocket. I looked at it and read those words that were growing oh, so familiar, by now: "For God does not give us the spirit of fear, but of power and of love and a sound mind."

10

Winning Is . . .
Having Patience until the Victory Comes

Quarterbacks always seem to be the point of conversation and sometimes the bone of contention in discussions about football. Mickey Elam had been a converted running back who had made a difference for us as the quarterback. A red-shirted freshman quarterback named Mike Brannon had made a difference in the 1979 season when he worked in concert with Mickey Elam.

Waiting in the wings was yet another quarterback, a young man who transferred to Baylor University from the University of Missouri. The decision to leave the football program at Missouri and come to Baylor University, where he had to pay his own way for a semester, was not as hard a decision for Jay Jeffrey as some people might imagine. First of all, he had very close Baylor ties. His father, James Jeffrey, had been an All-conference running back at Baylor in the 1950s. His brother, Neal Jeffrey, had led Baylor University to its first conference championship in fifty years in 1974. Jay felt that Baylor was the place for him. So he came and spent a year establishing his eligibility. Now he looked forward to the spring of 1980 when he might compete for the starting quarterback job.

The spring of 1980 passed quickly for me. Besides spring practice and preparing for the upcoming season, I went to Dallas every chance I got to visit with Kyle Woods. In the spare moments that were left, I sought and raised funds for Kyle's rehabilitation fund. I took extra speaking engagements so that I could put into the Kyle Woods Fund any honorarium I might receive. I was moved by a meeting that I had with a group of Dallas people who were not all Baylor graduates, but who were merely concerned about the life of the young athlete who had been injured.

A New Home for Kyle

As Kyle neared the end of his rehabilitation at Caruth Rehabilitation Center in Dallas, one problem became clearly evident to me. His mother and dad and younger brother lived in an apartment complex in Dallas. It was a tiny apartment for that many people. A narrow staircase went up to two upstairs bedrooms. It would be impossible for Kyle to negotiate those stairs or for his family to carry him up and down. He had to have a place to live where he could move around, use his wheelchair and enjoy some freedom. I told Anna I wanted her to start looking for a house in a good area, a house that would be suitable for Kyle and his future and for their family at this time. She began to look and after much searching found a place she liked. Kyle liked it too; I liked the neighborhood and the accessibility to the expressway.

In trying to get financing, someone put me in touch with an SMU man who ran a savings and loan. I met with him and explained our problem. He not only let us have the loan at a very reasonable rate, but before I left, he had contributed $100 to the fund. I walked out of his office thinking how truly great people can be. Jack Folmar, a very successful businessman in Dallas; Vic Salvino, another man who has great compassion for humanity; Hershel Forrester and many others in the Dallas area were instrumental in helping us raise the funds to get the house for Kyle Woods.

No sooner had we gotten the house than we realized another problem that would confront Kyle as he continued to progress. We wanted Kyle to have a bathroom where he could be totally self-sufficient. Some years hence when he might be alone we wanted him to be able to take care of himself. People from the realtors' organization in Dallas worked with us to develop and complete a bathroom for Kyle's house that he could use personally and discreetly. Largely through the help of these Dallas friends, Kyle Woods had one more vehicle to move him toward self-sufficiency. Also, it made me feel good to know that this young man and his family were being touched by a lot of people whom they didn't even know but who nonetheless cared about them as human beings.

Actually, on the way home from Dallas after arranging for the bathroom, I realized I felt better than I had in a long time. I was encouraged about Kyle and his needs being met, and I was excited about the upcoming season.

A Mature Response to a Problem

I took Donell home, drove to the office and started looking through my mail. On my desk was a sealed envelope from the athletic department, announcing to me that our athletic cafeteria would be cancelled for the upcoming year. I was astonished beyond words. We had worked hard recruiting young men who were expecting a cafeteria of their own, as football players at Baylor had had for decades. After slamming a few doors and letting my rage simmer down a bit, I sat down and looked at the situation calmly. First of all, I would not follow my first instinct and slap my resignation on the table; this was one more battle that I was going to fight and win. I had an obligation not only to the coaching staff and players but to the university as well, and no matter what the adversity I was going to find a way to get around it.

The best way I could think of to deal with this new crisis was through honesty. Our players had reported to the campus the opening day of the 1980 season. I met with our captain, Mike Singletary, who had been a consensus All-American his junior year, a two-time All-Southwest Conference selection and defensive player of the year in 1978 and 1979 in the Southwest Conference. He was a revered and respected leader of our team. I told Mike exactly what had happened and told him it was imperative that the team handle this with the proper attitude. A team that gets caught up in worries and concerns is not a team that can concentrate on what has to be done.

"The only way that we can make this season the kind of success that we want it to be is for the team members to make up their minds that they are not going to let this distract them," I told him. "From a schedule standpoint, it will be inconvenient to eat with nonathletes, but there will be some advantages. The students will get to know you. The food quality will be better than you expect. The problem will be the evening meal because we get off the practice field late and the campus cafeterias are already closed. There may be some cold meals and there may be some inadequate meals, but the key to the situation is how we handle it mentally."

I then asked Mike for his opinion. He looked directly into my eyes and said something that thrilled me. What he said was truly the mark of a leader. He said, "Coach Teaff, you explain it to the team as you've explained it to me and I assure you they will do whatever it takes to handle the situation. They trust you, and if you tell them something, they know that's the way it is. I can promise you from my vantage point as a captain that we will make it work."

Watching that 1980 team handle the adverse situations with which it was confronted—the cafeteria mixup, Kyle Woods and others—was a great lesson in the power of attitude and mind control. The members were determined that they were not going to let this one disturbance distract them. I knew by the way they were dealing with it that we had a special group of young men. Only time would prove how special they really were. They turned out to be the finest football team ever assembled from Baylor University. From start to finish they were a team with character.

Being at the Right Place

The tough times weren't totally over for me, but I had certainly come to the conclusion that what I was doing was right, the way I was doing it was right, and the place in which I was doing it was the place for me.

In early August when Jack Patterson, our athletic director, announced his retirement, some people thought that I would immediately seize the chance to become the athletic director of Baylor University and give up football. It seemed there were people who thought that this was my intention all along. But people who thought that never really understood me. I am a football coach and my desire is to work with young men. I did tell Dr. McCall and Dr. Reynolds that I would serve in both capacities, but I also told them that I would not want to give up football coaching to become the athletic director. I was asked to appear before the faculty athletic committee and I was thankful for that opportunity. I had been at Baylor University going into my ninth year and I had never had the opportunity to appear before that group. It was good for me to answer the committee's questions and clear up any misconceptions the members might have had about my goals and purposes at Baylor University. I told the faculty athletic committee the same thing I told Dr. McCall and Dr. Reynolds. I was told that the edict laid down by the trustees was that the head coach in any sport at Baylor could not simultaneously be the athletic director. I personally think that is a good rule and I concur with it.

I was very pleased with the university's decision to name Bill Menefee as athletic director. Bill had been the basketball coach at Baylor and was a very successful one at that. He had been with Baylor University a long time and was in the physical education department in charge of our marina on campus. He was an excellent administrator and a man with whom I would really enjoy working. Once the athletic director's job was settled, I was able to go into the football season with my mind totally on football and with an unusually good feeling about the upcoming season.

The Season That Counted

We had lost numerous players from the 1979 Peach Bowl championship team, so when the sports writers came through in late August, it didn't take them long to turn their eyes and attentions in another direction. In fact, they picked us to finish sixth in the Southwest Conference. I relayed that information to our team. When it was announced, the consensus among our team members was that it really didn't matter where we were picked at the beginning; it was how we finished the season that counted.

There were so many new faces on the squad that I was deeply concerned about having to play our first game against Lamar University in Beaumont. Lamar was a school trying to upgrade its athletic program. We had played the school in 1979 and we were playing Lamar again in 1980 in Beaumont. Larry Kennon, the Lamar head football coach, had been an assistant at SMU and was following in the footsteps of the public relations people who created Mustang Mania. He now had created Cardinal Craze. To tell you the truth, I was more than a little concerned about Cardinal Craze. We were playing on foreign soil and in a very small stadium compared to the ones in which we normally play. I knew it would be a hostile environment and, to be very frank, it was hard to get our team very high to play Lamar. So to put it bluntly, I prepared this team for the Lamar game as if we were preparing for the championship game.

I remember the kickoff well. Lamar received. Lamar's return man came up the right side of the field close to our bench area, broke to his left, sprinted down the sideline and was stopped on the seven-yard line. The people in the stands went absolutely berserk. You would have thought they had just beaten Baylor. Lamar's offensive team broke the huddle and came to the line of scrimmage. I could almost see the cold stare that Mike Singletary placed on that quarterback as he stepped up to take the snap. He took the snap, then turned and pitched the ball to the tailback. The tailback moved to his right and cut up toward the line of scrimmage. About three yards behind the line of scrimmage he was hit headon by Mike Singletary, 230 pounds of probably the greatest football player I'd ever coached up to that time. The ball went one way and the player went the other. The ball came back up field toward our bench 25 yards. That was the end of Lamar. The game ended with a score of 47–2 in favor of Baylor.

The game against West Texas State University had a unique flavor to it. Kansas State University had notified us that they would not play us. They were to be our second ball game of the 1980 season and they simply did not want this game to occur. One of my friends, Bill Yung, was the head football coach at West Texas State and I wanted to give his team a game with Baylor. We made some schedule changes with North Texas and West Texas became our second game. Bill had been an assistant with me at Baylor University during our first championship. I'm sure he had mixed emotions about coming into Baylor Stadium and playing a team he had helped develop. Having worked with Bill I was very fond of him and his family. But the competitor in all of us comes out and the closer it got to the West Texas game, the more I thought of it as a game and one that we certainly must win.

Bill and I talked on the Wednesday before the game. We decided that the teams would meet at the center of the field before the game. All the coaches would be there and we would bow together and have prayer. This is an unusual sight to see at major college football games, but I think it is a great sign. Both Bill and I felt totally comfortable with this and our players and coaches did as well. It was good to have that kind of fellowship before we played a very difficult ball game that we eventually won by a score of 43–15.

The next week we flew in drizzling rain to Lubbock, Texas. It continued to rain that night. I think the rain helped us a good bit because Texas Tech wanted to throw the football and didn't have much success. Charles Benson, a sophomore defensive end who had been converted from linebacker, had an outstanding night and burst onto the Southwest Conference scene like a meteor. He was named Southwest Conference Player of the Week and had eleven unassisted tackles, a majority of them behind the line of scrimmage, in his first ball game with Baylor University. He contributed greatly to our winning the football game by a score of 11–3.

The next week, the University of Houston, the defending Southwest Conference champions, came to Baylor Stadium. We had had some unbelievable football games with them for the four previous years. Each time UH had beaten us by a small margin in the fourth quarter and three of those times UH went on to win or tie the Southwest Conference championship. When we met UH again in Baylor Stadium in 1980, we jumped out ahead and never relinquished the lead, winning 24–12. It was a good feeling to have the game with the defending Southwest Conference champions behind us and a victory under our belts. Undefeated, with four victories, climbing in the national ratings, we were to play another undefeated team, the Southern Methodist University Mustangs. We had defeated them a year before in a very close ball game in Texas Stadium. With seven seconds to go, we had jumped ahead and won. SMU had smarted the entire season over that loss and they came into Baylor Stadium in 1980 with a full head of steam. Before we knew it, SMU was ahead 14–0 at the end of the first quarter.

Only a few seconds into the start of the second quarter, Jay Jeffrey faced a third down situation. He went to the line of scrimmage, called an audible, then raised up and threw the football directly into the arms of SMU's fine defensive back, John Simmons. All Simmons had to do was just skip into the end zone for a very easy touchdown. As SMU kicked its twenty-first point, I'm sure our fans in the stands felt this was going to be an awfully long night. Jay Jeffrey came to the sidelines with his head down, but as he approached me he raised his head and looked me in the eye. "Coach," he said, "are you gonna take me out of the game?"

I said, "Jay, what do you think I should do?" I should have expected his answer.

"Coach, leave me in. I'm a winner. I'll make up for that mistake. We're going to win the football game. You'll see. Just have faith and trust in me."

Almost laughing, I said, "Jay, I just know you have that feeling of confidence and I feel that kind of confidence in you as well. I believe in you; you're going to stay in the football game and we're going to win it."

I honestly don't know if I was trying to pump him up or pump me up, because things looked pretty bleak at the moment. But our offense really started moving in the second quarter and we scored fourteen points. We left the field with a great deal of momentum.

Coming back in the third quarter we took the opening kickoff and came out about seven yards on two plays. We fumbled the ball on the third down and SMU recovered. The Mustangs had great field position and whammo, they had their twenty-eighth point. To win we now had to play flawless football, and that's exactly what we did—we had a perfect second half, scoring 32 points for the game to SMU's 28. We walked off the football field an undefeated team, winning five straight ball games.

Having Character Is Important

In the dressing room after the game was over, I had my usual postgame press conference. I was asked the question immediately. "Coach Teaff, what do you think of this team?" I never hesitated in answering, because in the last moments of that game and as we walked off that football field, my description of that team kept ringing and ringing in my head. "Character," I said and repeated, "Character. You can describe this team with one word—character. You don't come from behind against a good football team unless you have character. It enables you to stick with your plans, to keep your poise and constantly believe that you've got a chance and that you're going to win."

That night when I arrived home I held Donell tightly for a moment and I whispered in her ear: "We're going to win the Southwest Conference Championship. We're going to win it." She looked at me, smiled happily and said, "I know we are, honey. I know we are."

The next week, as we drove to the Texas A&M game, my mind flashed back to the 1978 season when we were called "the best 0 and 5 team in America." Now, here we were two years later 5 and 0 and one of the best football teams in America. I believed that it was about time for this turnaround.

As we drove, I could see the clouds darkening in front of us. About ten miles outside of Bryan, Texas, it started to rain. By the time we got to the beautiful stadium at Texas A&M the downpour was unbelievable. I thought, "Well, this will pass in just a few moments." We went in for an hour, had our devotional and dressed. When I stepped outside the dressing room to look again, it was raining harder than it had been when it started. Rain has a tendency to equalize teams and A&M was not one with whom I especially wanted to be equal on that day. I wanted to be better than the Aggies were. They had a good solid football team and playing them in College Station is somewhat akin to playing Arkansas in Fayetteville—it's a tough duty. We had a lot of confidence in what we had done up to that point in the season, so we determined that we were not going to change our philosophy, nor our attack because of the rain.

We won the toss of the coin and chose to take the football. That in itself in the face of driving rain gave our team a strange kind of confidence. Then we started to play the best we could under the circumstances. Soon we were thirty-three yards from the Aggie goal line in a fourth down situation. Robert Bledsoe, who had broken the Baylor all-time scoring record in kicking, came onto the field to kick a field goal into the driving rain toward the north goal post. The wind and rain were blowing steadily into his face. You could hardly see the field from the sidelines because of the rain. The ball was snapped; it was down; it was up; and it was through the uprights. Everybody in the stadium must have been able to tell who was going to win the game that day. Walter Abercrombie had another one of his sensational games carrying the football, and we won 46–7.

We were now definitely well on our way to the championship.

The next week at Amon Carter Stadium in Fort Worth, we played Texas Christian University. This game, too, was in the rain. But it wasn't water that was pouring down. It was footballs. It seemed like TCU put that ball into the air about 100 times and caught about 75 of them. I knew TCU's statistics had not been extremely good, but they were certainly good on that day. We came away with the victory, 21–6, but we spent the whole game scared that we wouldn't make it.

By now we were becoming utterly exhausted. We'd been up for every game we had played. The next week we were to play San Jose State University. San Jose was a good team, but it certainly wasn't supposed to be the caliber of our Baylor Bears. I made a decision which some people construed as taking San Jose State too lightly. The decision may have had that effect on our team, but I can't say for sure. I decided to use all three of our quarterbacks in that game, rotating them by quarters. We had three very good quarterbacks who deserved to play and deserved to have a chance to sharpen their skills. Jay Jeffrey had played most of the games so far, David Magrum only sparingly and Mike Brannon even less. Whether my decision contributed to what happened or not I do not know. Nevertheless, the game began with Baylor jumping out to a fifteen-point lead. It could have gone to thirty the way we were playing. Then right before the half San Jose State scored. Then the opponents came back in the third quarter, got a turnover, and scored again. They went for two points and made them.

We were inside the ten-yard line on several occasions and turned the football over or failed to kick a field goal. Our kicker, Robert Bledsoe, had been injured in the TCU ball game. I was trying a walk-on kicker and he missed our first extra point. That certainly didn't fill me with confidence. So consequently, instead of going for the field goals when we were inside the ten-yard line, we would go for the touchdown or the first down. Unfortunately, we didn't make either.

There was something about that game that caused me to have a feeling after it was over that we just weren't supposed to win.

Late in the fourth quarter we were well ahead of San Jose State. We shut the opponents down, forced them to punt, then returned the punt about forty yards. We were on their twenty-five-yard line, ready to go in and just put their lights out.

But lo and behold the flags came drifting down softly to the Astroturf stadium floor, with referees claiming that we had roughed the kicker. Now, instead of our having a first down on the opponents' twenty-five, they had a first down on our twenty-five! They hit a pass and scored. Now we were behind; we tried to come back but we threw an interception and they scored again. The game was over and they won, 30–22. San Jose's players and coaching staff were absolutely jubilant. They stayed on the field for an hour after the game, celebrating and taking pictures of each other. If I hadn't felt so badly about our own loss, I would have been delighted for those guys from San Jose State. It really meant the world to them.

Oh, What Might Have Been!

The what-might-have-been started early in the newspapers and on radio and television the next week. On my call-in show on Monday night, most of the comments were, "Oh, if we hadn't lost that game, we surely would have been national champions. Oh, what might have been!"

It seemed that all week long as we were preparing for the University of Arkansas, a dark cloud hung over our heads. It was that ominous feeling that we let something very important get away from us. We knew that if we could beat the University of Arkansas we would be at least tied for the Southwest Conference Championship, and that the game would be televised by ABC. We had an excellent plan for the University of Arkansas and we were really in a good frame of mind. But still the dark cloud lingered.

The game was played on a beautiful, unseasonably warm November day. Kyle Woods was driven down from Dallas to see his first game in Baylor Stadium since he was injured. He was in the dressing room, seated in his wheelchair, when I called the players together. We had finished our team prayer, and I covered a few things briefly that I wanted the players to keep in mind as we took the field.

As I finished, I turned to Kyle and asked him if he had anything to say to the team before the Arkansas game. He said, "I sure do." I walked over behind Kyle and pushed him to the center of the room and stepped back behind him. He paused for a moment and then seemed to look every player in the eye. He said, "Here it is. You take a setback and you turn it into a comeback." Every player, every coach, every trainer, manager, doctor in the room knew instantly what he was saying. You can take all the San Jose State games that have ever been lost, you can take every defeat that Baylor has ever suffered in the past, and put them in a pile and they would be totally insignificant to the loss that Kyle had suffered.

Kyle's hands dropped to the arms of the wheelchair. They had no dexterity in them and they were still. He turned the thumbs inside, locking them on the arms of the wheelchair. I saw the muscles flex across his back. He had on a tank top shirt and his arms began to bulge as he strained, straightening his elbows, arching his back, lifting his hips, pushing downward on the chair with his hands and his arms lifting his body up. With one giant lunge he pushed forward and stood up. Almost instantly he started to topple, due to inadequate balance. Some teammates reached out and grabbed his right arm and steadied him. There he stood in the dressing room, to emphasize the point he just made, that "You can take a setback and turn it into comeback."

A Dramatically Punctuated Message

I've never heard a greater message nor seen it so dramatically punctuated. The players carried the message with them onto the field and that day Arkansas never had a chance! Our players turned the setback of San Jose into a great triumph, a great comeback against the University of Arkansas 42–15. ABC televised the game and it was seen by hundreds of thousands of people. Darrell Royal, the retired University of Texas coach, did the color on the television broadcast and his expert comments on the game and the way our players performed brought joy to the hearts of the Baylor people who could not attend.

It was a great victory and once again demonstrated the character of the 1980 Southwest Conference champions. That's the title we assumed the very next week in Rice Stadium by a score of 16–6. There was bedlam in the dressing room after the game was over and I just stood back and smiled comfortably as I watched our captains receive the invitation to play in the 1981 Cotton Bowl against a team yet to be named. Speculation was that it would be Notre Dame or Alabama. Personally, I hoped it would be Alabama. I wanted to play Alabama again to better our efforts against that team in Birmingham. Alabama was without question the premier team in the United States year in and year out—a team I wanted our men to play.

On the bus ride back to the airport, I looked around and saw smiles of happiness and contentment everywhere, but the one that really caught my eye was Walter Abercrombie. In high school he had never played on a winning team. Here he was about to be named the outstanding offensive player in the Southwest Conference for the 1980 season. He had just been part of a team that had cinched the conference championship by two ball games. The joy that was his was experienced by all of us.

In preparing for the Cotton Bowl, there was an air of confidence that I did not detect in 1974 as we prepared for Penn State. We were the fifth- or sixth-ranked team in the nation, depending on which poll you read, and we were about to play what I considered to be the Number 1 team in the nation. Now, Alabama had lost two ball games by close scores and was not considered a serious contender this year for the national title. But that did not keep Alabama from being the best football team in the land.

Our Cotton Bowl headquarters was the Anatole Hotel in Dallas, a beautiful, spacious hotel literally packed with Baylor people. The night before the ball game, a pep rally was held in the enclosed tennis court of the Anatole. I was to speak at the pep rally. About ten minutes before the rally was to begin, I walked to the elevator, went down to the lobby, into the back of the tennis complex but could go no further. It was an absolutely jammed madhouse. I just turned back around and went up to my room. Traffic was backed up all the way to downtown Dallas and the fire marshal absolutely went crazy as the Anatole filled to overflowing in both its main lobbies. The Baylor people were beside themselves.

Time passed quickly and soon we found ourselves in the Cotton Bowl dressing room raring to go onto the field. We walked down the tunnel entering the stadium from the south end. As we came into the stadium a deafening roar arose. The fans stood yelling and screaming. We started our warmup procedures. Then in walked Coach Bear Bryant. I spoke to him and walked to the north end of the field where the team was doing its drills. I stopped, looked up into the stands and slowly did a 360-degree turn. There was an entire sea of green and gold—72,000 strong, nationally televised on CBS, and our second appearance in the Cotton Bowl in six years. I was extremely emotional about the whole day and what it meant to me, the team and Baylor University.

The End of the Long, Hard Climb

As I looked up at that fantastic crowd waving green and gold pom-poms, tears began to stream down my cheeks. One of the coaches walked by and asked, "Are you OK, Coach?" I said, "Yeah, I'm great." The hard, long climb to respect, recognition and success at this moment was worth it. It was worth every heartbreak, every heartache, every painful moment.

I've never in my life wanted to win a game as badly as I wanted to win that game. But it was not to be. Alabama played like the great team it was. We had seven turnovers and Alabama played perfectly. In the fourth quarter, miraculously we were still in the game, 14–2. As the game wound down, Alabama scored its thirtieth point and ended up defeating the courageous, gallant and magnificent Baylor Bears 30–2. I was deeply hurt over the loss. I hurt for the players; I hurt for our program; I hurt for the Baylor people. As I faced the sports writers after the game, I didn't know what to do or what to say. I felt like crawling into a hole and pulling it in after me, but again I had to face the music.

That night at the press conference, Coach Bear Bryant of Alabama was most gracious. As we sat side by side behind the glare of the lights and the many microphones that had been shoved into our faces, he whispered into my ear, "Grant, don't feel badly about the loss today. Your team played real well." I said, "Coach, I can't help but feel badly."

The Bear said, "Listen, I probably hold the world record for lost bowl games." And then he smiled. What a great coach and what a gracious man! There in a moment of triumph, for a split second, he made me feel better. I thought to myself, "You know, I can probably never break his winning record, but to lose eight bowl games in a row is a record I could achieve and I wouldn't mind holding either."

After the press conference, I went back to the Anatole, took the elevator up to the sixteenth floor, and walked into my room. There, our family was gathered. My mom and dad, Donell's mom and dad, Donell's brother Rod and his wife Marilyn, my sister Juanez and her husband Carroll Carver were all gathered around the room. At a time like that no one really seems to know what to say, but leave it to a five-year-old to come up with the right words. As I walked into the room Chris, my nephew, looked up from his coloring book and said, "Bad game, Grant." I smiled at the sincerity with which he said it.

In December, right after the 1980 season, I had two contacts about the possibility of coaching at other schools. The president of Auburn University called and asked me to consider the coaching job there. I told him I was committed to Baylor, but he asked if I would meet with the Auburn search committee in Dallas the next week. I agreed and was really impressed with what they wanted in a program; however, I informed them that I would remain at Baylor. During the week of the Cotton Bowl, I met with the president and athletic director of another large state school. Boy, was that a tempting offer! I asked that school to give me until I got to Hawaii, where I was to help coach the Hula Bowl. Then I would give them my answer. They agreed.

Another Bowl, Another Lesson

As I left for Honolulu and the Hula Bowl, I felt such a great burden of responsibility for the loss to Alabama that I was feeling very sorry for myself again. The plane had just lifted off and we were heading west toward Los Angeles and ultimately Honolulu. Donell turned to me and said, "Hey, get your head up. When Baylor has been to 22 straight bowl games, I can assure you that whoever we play, we'll beat them 30 points too." She was referring to the fact that Bear Bryant had taken Alabama to 22 straight bowl games. This was our second bowl game in a row, our third in seven years. Her point was well taken. When we landed in Honolulu I called the waiting athletic director and told him I would remain at Baylor.

Two of our finest players, Mike Singletary and Doak Fields, were playing in the Hula Bowl game. It was a great pleasure to work with them one more time and it was an even greater pleasure when our underdog West squad defeated the East. The game was on national television and it made me feel better to get a victory under my belt again. We returned to Waco just in time for a banquet honoring the Baylor coaching staff. After accolades by the Alumni Association, the Bear Club, the administration, the City of Waco and others, I was asked to say whatever I felt.

I stood and said, "I feel extremely humble and very, very grateful today. This is a big day for our coaching staff and for our families. It means so much to be recognized with these honors, but it also means more to be loved, and we feel loved and we want to thank you for it.

"When we left the field at the Cotton Bowl, after the Alabama loss, I was very, very upset. I had gotten up that morning before the game and I went through the lobby in the hotel three or four times. I had told people I met that I wanted them to know that I did not duck out of the rally the night before. I told them I couldn't get into the room. But that experience at the rally was magnificent. When I couldn't get in, I stopped on the balcony and watched our people enjoy themselves. As I continued taking care of various final duties, I was grabbed by this person and that person and they would say words to me that touched me so they literally made me cry. On three different occasions, I went back to my room and sat and sobbed. I was very emotional that day with our team. I know that they thought I had lost my mind, but I couldn't help it.

"I think that morning of the game it dawned on me how extremely important our game with Alabama was. We had come so far in such a short time through much adversity. After the loss, it took me about three days to get into a position to where I could even enjoy being in Hawaii and enjoy the added bonus of coaching Doak and Mike and then finally winning the game.

"But then I received a letter after the Cotton Bowl that helped me sum up everything I felt. Let me share it with you tonight:

Dear Coach Teaff,

For the last two hours since our defeat by the University of Alabama, I have been depressed, angry, hurt and choked up with a variety of negative feelings. My wife has been on the verge of tears. My Baylor daughter and her roommate have been blue and despondent. I have talked to a half dozen of my Baylor friends about our defeat that we just suffered in the Cotton Bowl. For almost two hours I have felt that the entire season was a dismal failure because of the whipping administered to our boys by the Alabama team. While pouting and brooding in my easy chair, it suddenly dawned on me what actually happened. I was complaining because the Baylor Bears did not win the Cotton Bowl game. I was depressed because we only won the conference and did not vanquish Bear Bryant's Alabama. How short my memory is. Having been a student and gone through the frustrating years of football in 1950–54, I was so thrilled when we won the conference in 1974. In the past, we came so close but could never quite make it. I had given up years ago the hope of ever winning the championship, so imagine my unbelieving joy in 1974 when the miracle occurred. I didn't expect to beat Penn State in the Cotton Bowl that year, and was not the least bit disappointed when we lost because we had won the conference. I knew that I would never see us win another championship in my lifetime, and it didn't really matter because we had done it once. Now, six years later you and the Baylor Bears have done it again and so convincingly this time. I now find myself upset because we didn't win the bowl game, only the conference championship. That tells me how far the Baylor football program has come in these few short years. We have now reached the place where a Cotton Bowl defeat angers us. We have reached the place where we really believe that Baylor can do it. We have reached the place that no more miracles are necessary to win the championship, to go 10–2 and so forth. Despite our loss today, I realize we have now arrived, that Baylor will now begin to go to bowls, not always the Cotton Bowl on a regular basis, and win our share of them. I'm ashamed of my anger, as temporary as it was. I now realize that Baylor football has arrived. We are proud of you all, and if you will, you will take us back to the Cotton Bowl and next time we'll win.

(Signed) J. David Cox, Nacogdoches, Texas

"That letter sums it up real well. I had the same emotions, the same feelings. I hated to lose, but there'll be another time. We thank God for the privilege of being a part of this football program."

I turned and faced the area where Dr. McCall, Dr. Reynolds and Bill Menefee were sitting and said, "Donell and I have made a commitment to Baylor and will remain here until we are no longer wanted or until we feel God wants us to do something else."

As we drove home that night after the banquet, Donell snuggled close to my side and I put my arm around her, and said, "You know, honey, Dr. Reynolds, Dr. McCall and all the people that I came in contact with tonight after the dinner really made me feel great. They expressed great pleasure in the commitment that we have made. I feel a great sense of peace about that decision to stay at Baylor University and about our future here. It may be a while before we have a year to equal the 1980 season, but there will be other years, other goals to reach, other young men to see develop and mature and become what God had intended for them to become."

Then I asked her, "Do you remember the last paragraph in *I Believe*? It says something like, seasons will come and seasons will go, some good and some bad, but I believe that the thrill of sharing, loving and growing in a God-centered life reaches far beyond the won and loss record."

Donell raised her head and nodded, remembering.

11

Winning Is . . .
Learning to Be Humble

No matter how many successes I've had in life, something ultimately comes along that keeps me very humble and will prioritize my life for me if I don't do it myself first.

In the 1975 season, after our first Southwest Conference championship in 1974, that great humbling agent was the unusual number of fumbles we experienced in 1975. In fact, we led the conference in the number of fumbles that occurred in our games. That spring and summer when I went around the state talking to Baylor groups, I knew they would ask about this high number of fumbles. So I was ready for them: I told them that a Waco minister, while leading the opening prayer for the 1975 season, made an entreaty of God that he thought would be appropriate in light of our 1974 successes. He prayed, "God, make us humble." I contended that God misunderstood and thought the preacher said, "God, make us fumble."

This same type of humbling experience occurred again in the summer of 1981, following our two unbelievable years—1979 and 1980—when the Baylor Bears led the Southwest Conference in total victories, played in two bowl games and had unprecedented success in terms of All-America and All-Conference players. It was a heady time for all of us. But in late July, 1981, as I was leaving the First Baptist Church of Waco, one of the local bank presidents stopped Donell and me at the door. He wanted us to meet his young sons. He said to them, "Boys, I want you to meet the greatest coach in America." One of them, a five-year-old redhead named Joe, extended his hand toward me and asked, "Are you really Tom Landry?"

A Bigger Slice of Humble Pie

The opening game of the 1981 football season, I received an even larger piece of humble pie. Lamar University made short work of defeating the defending Southwest Conference champions and brought us back to earth in a hurry. At the conclusion of the game, I wished that I were Tom Landry—or anyone else for that matter except Grant Teaff. I felt miserable.

The 1981 season was pretty well summed up by one football game played in Little Rock, Arkansas, on a crisp late October evening. The lead in the game changed hands several times, and with only a few minutes to go, we scored and went ahead. Arkansas completed a couple of scrambling desperation passes, got itself in field goal range and scored a field goal to win 41–38 as the clock ran out. The game was seen on national TV and replayed throughout the week on the sports network. As I stepped away from the game and looked back at it objectively, it was one of the finest college football games that I have ever seen, but it was also typical of the 1981 season. The outcomes were all close, but not close enough. We finished the season with a 5–6 record.

A Welcome Staff Addition

Then, in the spring of 1982, a man came to our coaching staff who started making a tremendous difference in our entire athletic program. This hiring of our strength coach, Bob Fix, had its roots in a story that goes all the way back to 1957 when I took the track and football coaching job at McMurry College under Tommy Ellis. Having never run track, I was totally open as to training and developmental methods. I was soon convinced that the use of weight training could be important in the physical development of a track or football athlete. We did not have the money at McMurry to buy weights, so I made some out of one- and five-gallon food containers that came from the college cafeteria. I filled these cans with concrete and stuck into the concrete a two-inch galvanized pipe. When I pulled the cans away, the concrete weights remained.

I began to study all forms of muscle development. Isometric training came into vogue and we built apparatuses to send all our athletes through that kind of development. I developed harnesses and hooked those to ski ropes attached to large tractor tires, trying to develop the leg power of my track men. Then as I learned the fundamentals of running, I developed a running improvement program, getting each youngster to use the fundamentals of running—the carrying of the arms, the eyes straight ahead, the lifting of the knees, the placement of the feet, the relaxation of the jaw.

I incorporated that into our football training as well. In fact, I'm sure one of the reasons J. T. King offered me the job at Texas Tech in 1966 was that he had heard me lecture on the off-season weight training and running development programs. One of the first things he had me do at Texas Tech was to put in the off-season philosophy.

When I went to Angelo State in 1969, one of the first things I asked of that school's president, Dr. Lloyd Vincent, and athletic director, Phil George, was to be able to build a facility for off-season training, and they allowed me to do that. We designed a unique place which was beautiful and extraordinary for weight-training.

A New Weight-training Program

Coming to Baylor University in 1972, I was immediately shocked at the small size, weakness and low endurance level of the players. In the spring of 1972, the first thing we did was initiate a detailed and strong off-season development program. We developed the circuit theory that is now widely used. The theory would allow forty to fifty players to work for about forty minutes to an hour rotating from one exercise to another every three minutes on a whistle. It not only built up the strength but also the cardiovascular system and got a lot of people through their off-season workout program in a hurry.

The other thing that shocked me at Baylor University was that the school just didn't have any weight room facilities. There was one small twelve-foot-by-fifteen-foot room that had one universal gym in it. So we immediately built a facility and started using free weights. Over the years, I have either trained someone on my staff to do weight training or handled it myself.

My third year at Baylor University, a young man from Michigan walked into my office and told me he would like to be a part of our program. The man, Bob Fix, had heard me speak at a Michigan clinic the previous year. I did not have any part-time or graduate assistant openings at that time.

Bob told me that he and his wife Karen and two small boys were willing to bite the bullet, move to Texas and become part of our program without any remuneration. As incredible as that may sound, this happens quite often with people who want their chance to get into college coaching. Some are even willing to start out as a volunteer to do so. So, I took Bob at his word and put him into a volunteer position.

A Vietnam veteran, Bob Fix at that time weighed 165 pounds and was quiet and introverted. In fact, for the first year I hardly heard Bob say a word, but he was a hard worker and did what he was asked to do. The next year I was able to put him on as a part-time coach with a minimal salary.

Even though Bob was introverted, I noted that he communicated very well with individual players. In fact, one young man, Max McGeary, came to Baylor as a totally unheralded and unsought football player and turned out to be an All-Conference defensive end. He can probably trace his turnaround to Bob Fix.

Not only did Bob work with Max in the off-season program and in the weight facility, he encouraged him and affirmed him constantly, which the young man sorely needed. His father had died in an accident a year or so earlier, and Max felt he needed to go to a school where people really cared about him.

Bill Hicks, who was recruiting in West Texas that year, said he had found a young man in Denver City, Texas, who played fullback and linebacker and who badly wanted to come to Baylor University. He neither had the speed to play fullback nor the size to play linebacker, but at Bill's insistence we invited Max down for a visit. I told him bluntly that we did not have a scholarship to offer him but that we would keep him in mind. He sat across from me with tears streaming down his cheeks and said, "Coach, please give me consideration. I want to come to Baylor University and you'll never regret it."

A Wise Recruiting Choice

As we neared the end of recruiting season, Bill Lane and I were in Dallas interviewing an outstanding young man who was one of Texas' blue chip high school players and who was still considering Baylor University along with some other schools. But just after we entered his home, his mother approached me and flat out asked if we could help her son get a car if he chose Baylor University. Miffed but trying hard to be gracious, I said good-bye and went back to my car with Bill. I immediately thought of the contrast between this scene and the situation with Max. I realized there was a young man in Denver City who wanted to come to Baylor University while we were sitting in front of the home of a guy who wanted us only if we could give him a car. I drove to a phone booth and called Max to tell him the news. I'm sure people within miles of Denver City could hear him yell when I told him I had a full scholarship for him.

Well, Bob Fix took Max under his wing and turned him into the direction of using the talent he had. Max came to me and said, "Coach Teaff, I really want to be on the specialty teams. I can block kicks for you." So the next year, Max McGeary blocked eleven kicks by himself. We took one of his blocked kicks against SMU, marched it to the other end of the field and kicked a field goal to come out winners in that crucial football game. Ron Meyers of SMU had never had a field goal blocked in his coaching career, but Max blocked two in one game that day.

Max went on to become an All-Conference defensive end for us, playing outstanding football and displaying physical toughness equal to any I've known. Max is a coach now and coaches with the same intensity that he played. You can rest assured that he is caring about young men in the way that Bob Fix cared for him.

I knew from the experience with Max that Bob Fix was someone special and had some characteristics that we needed. I called

Bob in and told him that rather than become a major college coach, I thought he should become an athletic strength coach—one who would know all about strength and physical development and would be able to teach it and stay up with it. This was the coming wave in college athletics, I told him. I asked him to take over our strength program as a graduate assistant and offered to send him anywhere to study and learn from anyone who knew anything about weight training. So for a couple of years, Bob did that, all the while continuing to suffer financially.

After a couple of years, Bob felt he needed to go back to Michigan, to be nearer his family there and to get into high school coaching. So he left, but I knew that someday I would have a chance to bring Bob back to Baylor because of his deep and abiding love for the school. A short time later, in 1980, Bob moved back to Texas. By that point I had no openings on my staff and I had, in fact, hired a full-time strength coach. Bob took a job at Midway Junior High School, in a community on the outskirts of Waco.

Then in 1982, I had the opportunity to hire a new strength coach, and called Bob immediately. He is a person who does not just tell a player how to do something; he does it with him. And so, in developing one of the finest strength programs in America today, Bob has become one of the finest looking and strongest strength coaches in the country. In a period of about a year, Bob went from about 180 pounds to 220 pounds. He never asks an athlete to do an exercise he has not first done with the athlete. And he continues to have superb rapport with the players, as best evidenced by an incident in 1982 which caused a change in our season and in Bob as well.

That Downward Spiral Again

During the 1982 season, that downward psychological spiral I've referred to earlier returned again. I saw that 1982 team really disintegrate to the lowest point I've ever seen in my coaching career. Texas Christian University's football team, which had only defeated us one time since I had been at Baylor, trounced us in Fort Worth, 38–14. Then when we played Tulane in the Superdome, I felt like we just quit. It's one thing to lose a game

30–15, but it's something else to lose when you feel like you didn't give it your best. In fact, I was so upset that it took me about 30 minutes before I could talk to the players or the news media. I went into a shower stall in the dressing room and sat down and hurt all over.

As we flew back to Waco, I was sure the folks up in Fayetteville, Arkansas, were snickering at us because they had just moved up to the Number 5 spot in the country, were undefeated and their next opponents were those pitiful Baylor Bears who had just lost to a very poor Tulane team. The closer we got to home, the angrier I became. I was totally convinced that this year's problem was one of mental toughness—when things started turning bad we just weren't tough enough to turn it back around. The personality of each team is always different, and each must be dealt with differently. Some teams respond best to praise; others must be dealt with more drastically. It was obvious that this team needed a drastic approach.

At the Sunday afternoon meeting with the players, I just told them flat out how I felt. I said I was very glad that there was not a gang fight in the stadium that night because I feared I would look over and see a bunch of our players cowering beneath the bench. If I could find eleven men who would fight for the full sixty minutes the next weekend, I told them, I believed we would beat the University of Arkansas. But, I told them I doubted that I could find eleven such warriors.

Monday morning at staff meeting, I told the coaches that we were going to scrimmage every day of the week until we found some defensive people who would hit and some offensive people who would come off the football and attack the opposing team. I told Bob Fix, "In that weight room, make them be intense and tough in everything that they do."

Normally we don't work out on Mondays on the football field. The players come over and go through their rehabilitation for their bumps and bruises, then go to their weight program and then to the study hall. But this Monday was different. The entire team was suited in full pads on the field, with an hour-and-a-half workout in full pads and then an hour of scrimmage. We put the Number 1 offensive team versus the Number 1 defensive team; the Number 2 offensive team against the Number 2 defensive team; and so on. They looked terrible. The offense was awful and the defense couldn't make a tackle. We all left the field sick at heart.

But when the players got to the weight room that afternoon, they heard an unusual lecture from Bob Fix. He told them he was sure they would not win against Arkansas but that if they did, the team could shave off all the hair on his head. Now, that wasn't saying much because Bob was bald on top and had only a fringe of hair around the sides of his head and down the back. Nevertheless, this promise caught the attention of the players.

Throughout the week we continued the same format: the workouts were tougher, more intense and harder each day, and they produced the same terrible results. On Thursday, we were sort of stumbling and bumbling along as we had been all week. It appeared the week's efforts had been useless. Then all of a sudden, a linebacker made an absolutely beautiful head-on tackle that popped and reverberated throughout the stadium. The defensive tackle jumped up and down and started screaming, "Way to hit, way to hit." Then the defensive back picked the linebacker up and lifted him into the air, yelling and screaming, and all of a sudden the defense was ignited. The offense never got to the line of scrimmage that afternoon. Then the offense began to fight and believe in themselves. Excitement and enthusiasm for what they were doing began to arise. By late Friday, I felt we were ready to play the University of Arkansas.

I don't think I've ever had a team play a tougher and more aggressive football game than those Bears played that afternoon. At halftime everybody felt wonderful. I stepped up on a bench and yelled to the players that there were two things I wanted that afternoon: 1) a victory, and 2) Bob Fix's hair lying in the center of the dressing room floor immediately after the game. The players yelled, cheered and took off for their victory. And it was a great victory. We won 24–17.

Sure enough, when I got back to the dressing room, the players were yelling, "We want Fix's hair. We want Fix's hair." I turned to Bob, and he stood in the corner with a sheepish grin. One of the trainers had the razor that is used to shave off the ankles of the players before they are taped. The captains and all the players moved in on Bob and started taking his hair off. And I mean, they took it off in a hurry. From that day to this, Bob has never let that hair grow back. His bald head remains a symbol to the team of what they can accomplish and what they can do when they fight and are aggressive and mentally tough.

That event has also changed Bob a lot. Now he looks like Mr. Clean—muscular, baldheaded, but always with that warm, friendly smile.

A Surprising Change in Bob Fix

The change in Bob's personality from the introverted young man of several years ago reached its peak at the beginning of the 1983 season. We were playing Brigham Young University, a team that had had an exciting series of years under LaVell Edwards. It was one of those offensive shows that fans love to see. In the third quarter, we were on a drive and would go ahead of BYU if we scored. As I walked along the sidelines, I felt something hit me across the back of my head. I turned and saw Bob Fix looking up to the west side of the stadium swinging a towel over his head, and it was his swinging towel that had just popped me. I had put Bob on the sideline because the players enjoyed having him there, and I also needed him for sideline control. I had asked Bob to make sure the players stayed behind the coaching box. But when I looked up, he was leading yells and swinging a towel, and it really upset me. Here we were in the throes of trying to win a game against this great football team, and Bob Fix had nothing to do but lead yells. This went on for the rest of the game. Each time he hit me with the towel, I'd yell, "Bob, get back and keep that towel from hitting me." We won the game 40–36.

On Sunday afternoon as I went over my plans for the upcoming week, I was thrilled with the BYU victory but I was still miffed at Bob for his sideline conduct. I made up my mind that Monday afternoon I would have Bob in after workout and speak to him sternly about this. But when I got home that night, I had three or four phone calls from Waco people about how they appreciated what Bob Fix had done for the folks on the west side of the stands, which is opposite from the student side where the yell leaders stay. The folks on the west side are the moms, dads and alumni, and they felt it was the first time that anybody

had encouraged them to be a part of the victory. The next morning, I received six or seven telegrams from the Dallas and Houston
areas, saying the same thing. "Great idea having Bob Fix lead
all of us in a yell. We think it helps."

I decided to delay my talk with Bob for a day so I could try
to put all this in perspective. But in the next day's mail came
even more favorable comments about Bob Fix. There were nearly
a hundred letters from all over the state praising that bald-headed
coach on the sidelines.

So on Tuesday night, I called Bob in finally and told him,
"If you're going to swing that towel on the sidelines and lead
yells, just stay away from me. That's all I ask. Keep up the
good work."

Since that time, he's been on the sidelines, and he is now recognized all over the nation because the TV cameras can't resist
zooming in on him. That quiet, introverted and humble Bob
Fix is now a full-fledged cheerleader, a 220-pound world-class
strength coach from Baylor University.

The 1979 Coaching staff (Peach Bowl team):
Front Row: Wade Turner, John O'Hara, Head Coach Grant Teaff, Corky Nelson, Joe Broeker
Back Row: Duke Christian, Bill Lane, Skip Cox, Cotton Davidson, Billy Mills, Bill Hicks

Grant and Donell Teaff

Mike Singletary and Coach Teaff

Jay and Neal Jeffrey

Bear Bryant and Coach Teaff

Walter Abercrombie in action

Bob Fix before and after

Bob Fix the cheerleader

Kyle Woods

Brad Bradley ph

Walter Payton, Kyle Woods and Coach Teaff at the Dallas All-Sports Banquet, 1985

Kyle Woods on the sideline

Alfred Anderson

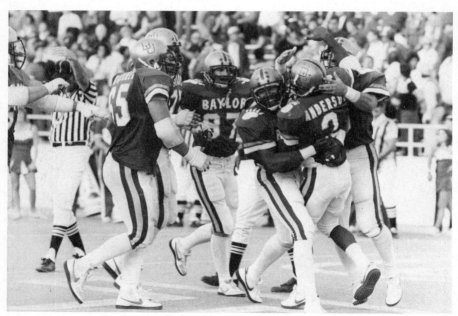

Anderson on the receiving end of an exciting 60-yard pass

GRANT TEAFF

BAYLOR UNIVERSITY

The Baylor Bears' Coach Teaff

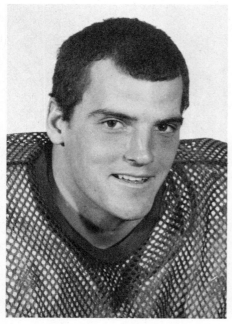

Scott Smith

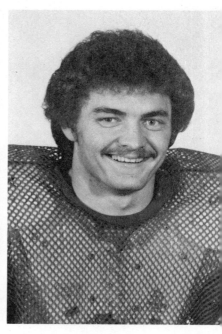

Mickey Elam

Philip Kent

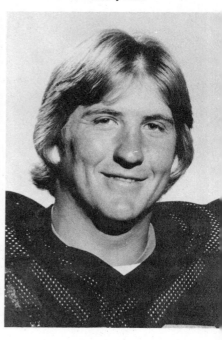

Mark Jackson

Winning the Peach Bowl trophy, 1979

Kent Townsend

Mark Adickes

Tammy and her husband, Russ Bookbinder

12

Winning Is . . .
Being Able to Face Tomorrow

After Kyle Woods was injured, I tried to do everything that I could to help him face all his uncertain tomorrows. Because of so many caring people both in the Baylor University family as well as outside of it, Kyle's medical bills have been taken care of and he and his family have a home in Dallas equipped for his many special needs. The Kyle Woods Trust Fund continues to help support him and people still contribute to it. Thanks to the tireless efforts of his therapists and family, Kyle is now back to his playing weight and able to do more for himself than we ever thought would be possible. He even has a telephone sales business that he operates from his home.

Every time I go to Dallas and drive up to Kyle's house, I think of what he told me the day we bought his house. He was smiling his biggest smile, and he motioned for me to sit beside him. He said, "Coach, do you remember when you taught my freshman class how to set goals?" I said, "Yes, of course." Kyle's lower lip quivered as he said, "One of my goals was to get an education so I could buy my mom and dad a home." He smiled again and said, "I got it a lot quicker and in a different way than I ever dreamed. But I reached my goal." I couldn't speak, so I just nodded my head.

The strain of Kyle's crisis was just beginning to lessen for me and I was able to go through my day to day activities without constantly thinking of this young life hanging in the balance when another bone-chilling trauma occurred in my own family.

A Heart-rending Phone Call

During the past few years, I have served on the Nike Coaches Advisory Board. We meet once a year in some nice location to talk about athletics and athletic equipment. In March, 1982, Donell and I were winging our way to San Juan, Puerto Rico, where we would catch a shuttle flight to the Island of St. Thomas to meet other coaches and their wives for a week at a beautiful resort. Upon arriving at the resort, we walked to the registration area. We were immediately handed a note to call Cotton Davidson, one of my assistant coaches. When I'm on vacation, a call from the office immediately signals a problem and this was no exception, because the note bore the word, "Urgent!" When I finally reached Coach Davidson on the phone, I could tell he was nervous and anxious. He quickly told me why. "Coach, Tammy has had a problem up in Dallas, and you and Donell need to get back right away," he said. My heart sank as I thought of my oldest daughter, and I quickly asked what the situation was.

He went on, "Coach, it looks very serious. They are not sure but they think she has had a brain hemorrhage. Her blood pressure has gone sky high and she has lost her vision. She was taken to a Dallas hospital this morning after having lost her sight while driving on an expressway in Dallas."

Cotton told me that his information was very limited, but he understood she was being taken to surgery. The doctors were advising that Donell and I return to Texas immediately. He said my brother-in-law, Dr. Carroll Carver, an oral surgeon in Arlington, Texas, was enroute to the hospital at that moment to check on Tammy's condition. He suggested that I shortly call Carroll at the hospital. I told Cotton that we would return to Texas as quickly as we could.

I wasted no time in informing Donell of the news. We immediately tried to arrange for a flight to Dallas and discovered the isolation of the Caribbean islands. The next flight out of St. Thomas was not until the next morning. Even then we had to fly to San Juan, Puerto Rico, before going on to Dallas. It would be at least twenty-four hours before we could get to Dallas.

In ordinary circumstances, such an isolated setting would be enjoyable, but under these conditions we were miserable. Fortunately, we were able to use the telephone, but it was hard to get through to Medical City Hospital in North Dallas.

We checked into our beautiful condo overlooking the Caribbean, but could hardly enjoy the view. There were two couples assigned to each condo, and fortunately we were sharing our quarters with LaVell Edwards of BYU and his wife, Patti, two very lovely and understanding people. In this moment of crisis, they became our close confidants and supporters.

Finally we reached Carroll Carver and found out that he and my sister, Juanez, had spent the entire day with Tammy in the hospital. He had cancelled his own appointments to be with Tammy. Carroll told us that in the operating room the doctors performed a spinal tap but could find no trace of a hemmorhage. He said they were now focusing on Tammy's extremely high blood pressure.

Carroll also filled us in on the events surrounding Tammy's illness. He said she was driving down the expressway in North Dallas on her way to work that morning when suddenly without warning her vision had blurred and she was unable to focus on anything. She had the presence of mind to follow the blurred image of the car in front of her, finally following it off the expressway at an exit. Miraculously, that car exited right in front of the apartment complex where a young man whom Tammy had been dating lived. She cautiously worked her way to the front door of his apartment. He was late for work that morning and was still at home. He opened the door to find Tammy pleading, "I can't see. I can't see." He immediately rushed her to the closest hospital. Dr. Ralph Greenlee, a neurosurgeon, was the attending physician on call in the emergency room that morning, and he ordered the spinal tap because he feared a hemorrhage. Dr. Treavor Mabrey, a wonderful physician, ministered to Tammy and prayed with her.

Carroll said that a blood clot had been ruled out. He said there were other possibilities, including an aneurysm or a brain tumor. Donell and I spent the night on the island faced with those various extremes. Before we caught the plane the next day, we placed about ten calls to Dallas to check on the situation and to make arrangements for our speedy trip from the Dallas airport to the hospital.

We were picked up at the Dallas/Fort Worth Airport by close friends Bill and Lou White and driven immediately to the hospital. Racing down the corridor to the intensive care unit where Tammy was housed, we came upon our other daughters, Tracy and Layne. When they saw us, we all four broke into tears. Our daughters are all very different in personalities and tastes, but they share a love for one another that many parents can only wish for their children. Tracy and Layne had rushed to Dallas immediately to be with their sister and had been there for the twenty-four hours that we were trying frantically to get to Tammy's side.

Further down the hall, we met Tammy's physician, Dr. Greenlee. He said he still did not know the cause of Tammy's loss of sight nor the reason for the extremely high blood pressure. A nurse motioned us to Tammy's cubicle in that intensive care unit. The lights were dim, but as we stepped in Tammy called out "Mom? Dad?" and we said, "Yes, we are here." The three of us burst into tears. Tammy's eyes were covered with patches and the sight frightened us. Otherwise, she seemed OK except for her highly restricted movement.

"I'm glad you're here," she said. "I wanted you here so badly. But Mom, Dad, God is real. Even while you were so far away, I was not alone. God says He'll be with you all the time and He's been with me every moment."

Donell and I were grateful for those words and were amazed at the depth of the faith of this young, sick daughter of ours.

Dr. Mabry was most gracious to us during this period of time. He offered us the use of his office. We were surrounded by the love and concern of our friends and family. We received cards, letters, phone calls and personal visits from hundreds of people, including Baylor administrators, faculty members, students, football players, alumni, trustees and fans. John Wood, our new pastor in Waco, and several friends from First Baptist flew to Dallas to spend time praying and visiting with us.

As the week progressed, the doctors slowly eliminated the various possibilities. They said it was not an aneurysm. Then they said it was not a brain tumor. Finally we were told that there was some speculation that Tammy had multiple sclerosis. When we were first told of this possibility, MS did not seem as ominous as the other possibilities which now had been eliminated. Later, as the disease was confirmed, we learned more of its ramifications.

Despite our pain over what was transpiring, we still continued to marvel at the depth of Tammy's faith and the support of our friends. The way Tammy handled the situation confirmed to us that we had brought her up to have a deep and abiding faith in God. The outpouring of love from so many of our friends at Baylor University confirmed for us how right it was to be at this school doing what we have been called to do.

Despite the eventual diagnosis of MS and the possibility of continued deterioration of her physical health, Tammy has been able to lead a fairly normal life so far. After she was released from the hospital and had recuperated, I helped her obtain a job with the Dallas Mavericks. Tammy loves athletics, so this turned out to be the perfect choice.

Even more, this choice turned out to be a part of God's plan for Tammy's life. While working with the Mavericks, she met Russ Bookbinder. Russ and Tammy fell in love and married and now have a wonderful Christian home in Denver where he is vice-president for the Denver Nuggets, another professional basketball team. Tammy and Russ are coping well with the diagnosis of MS, and their faith continues strong. They have a positive attitude toward life as well as Tammy's illness. They face tomorrow with hope and promise.

On the Wings of Eagles

I have always tried to teach my players and my own children to do the best they can with what they have. That means taking all you possess, in terms of physical capabilities, knowledge, expertise and intangibles, and using them to the maximum.

The theory is that each day a person's performance should reach a higher level because he should improve in one or more areas. Obviously everyone is on a different level of performance; however, recognizing the need to improve is essential.

In the early 1980s, I came up with a way to emphasize and then recognize that cherished level of performance. I started the Eagle Wing Award. The Eagle Wing was to become the symbol for excellence in performance. The eagle soars above all other creatures, with power and majestic beauty. Our goal was to be like the eagle, climbing higher and higher with our performances. Isaiah 40:31 (KJV) explains that by waiting upon the Lord, we can gain strength, power and endurance, like the eagle: They that wait upon the Lord shall renew their strength; they shall mount up with wings as eagles; they shall run and not get weary; and they shall walk and not faint."

When I announced the award to the players, I told them (1) every player on the squad was eligible; (2) the award would be made after each game, during the season; (3) the award would consist of a pair of miniature eagle wings and a personal letter from me; (4) there would be no media recognition for the award; (5) the selection would be a judgment call by me and (6) my decision would be based on each player's performance during the week of workout and the game, if he played.

During the season on Sunday nights and Monday afternoons, I re-studied game film, went over my notes from the previous week's workouts and then made my decision as to the recipients of the Eagle Wing Awards for that week. On Tuesday, prior to the players' arrival, I went into the dressing room and placed the eagle wings on the back of the helmets. Then I would leave a personal letter in each winner's locker. In the letter, I explained why I was citing them and why I thought their performance was the highest they were capable of attaining at that point in their lives. Then I explained what they needed to do to reach a higher level. Each week, scout teamers, specialty men, back-ups and starters would walk into the dressing room, anxious to see if they had eagle wings on their helmets. It has proven to be an effective way to get the players aware of their own potential.

When Expectations Mesh

In the 1983 game against BYU, we unveiled our new "I" formation. We moved to the "I" from the Split Back because of a young man by the name of Alfred Anderson. Alfred was a Waco boy who was a blue chip football player from Richfield High School. He was sought by just about every school in the country, including Texas A&M, SMU and the University of Oklahoma. He told me that he chose Baylor University because he wanted to obtain a quality education and at the same time play ball for people who really cared about him as a person. I really admired Alfred and I appreciated his choosing our program from among some of the top schools in the country.

Though he was a quarterback in high school, we switched

Alfred to a running back during his freshman year in college. Our quarterback slots were filled, and I felt like he would be an excellent back-up choice behind running back Walter Abercrombie, the leading rusher in the Southwest Conference. Alfred became our designated scorer. We've run the power "I" formation inside the ten-yard line and for short yardage plays for the past twenty years. We call it a tandem offense. It is two tight ends, a tailback, a set halfback right behind the right offensive tackle and, of course, a fullback directly behind the quarterback. Walter Abercrombie played the tailback and Alfred Anderson as a freshman played the set halfback. From that position, he scored nine touchdowns during his freshman year.

Walter was back playing again in 1981, so I decided to get Alfred on the field where he could be a starter. I moved him to flankerback, and as a sophomore, Alfred played as a starter in that position. We allowed him to carry the ball from that position and he was also an excellent receiver. Then in 1982, Alfred Anderson became a starting left halfback and had an excellent year. Because of his strength and power, I decided to move to the "I" formation for the 1983 season. This turned out to be a good decision, and Alfred Anderson became a 1,000-yard rusher and Baylor led the Southwest Conference in total offense that year.

For Alfred, each new year brought new challenges and new horizons to conquer.

A Little Bitty Defensive Back

I was recruiting Alfred Anderson at the same time that I first heard about Gerald McNeil, a player who did a marvelous job overcoming some physical limitations. At 5-foot-6, Gerald weighed only 139 pounds. I was so unsure about his size that I first wrote him off as a candidate for our team, assuming that anyone his size would quickly be severely mangled on the college football field. Cotton Davidson, one of my assistant coaches, kept insisting that I not be so hasty in my judgment of Gerald's skills. He persuaded me to attend a high school game in which Gerald McNeil played for Killeen, Texas, and Alfred Anderson played for the opposing Richfield team. Alfred was sensational, but I was also extremely impressed with that little bitty defensive back named Gerald McNeil. I remember telling Cotton Davidson to go ahead and recruit Gerald because "he is tougher than the back end of a shooting gallery."

When they reported as freshmen in 1980, Alfred and Gerald were among the better athletes we had selected. They soon had chances to prove their abilities. We put Gerald McNeil into the position of our wide receiver rather than a defensive back. This was the position he played in that crucial 1980 game against the University of Houston. It was third and 15 on a must drive. Alfred Anderson was our back-up halfback in that game. Substituting, he threw a crucial halfback pass. Just as Alfred got hit, he turned loose of the ball and it seemed to flutter into the air and come down about twenty yards away. At first it looked as if it would fall to the turf incomplete. Then suddenly, seemingly from out of nowhere, tiny Gerald McNeil extended his arms, did a belly flop and caught the ball on the tips of his fingers. It was a beautiful catch! That combination play led to a victory over Houston and to two brilliant football careers at Baylor University. In their senior year of 1983, when they led our team to the Bluebonnet Bowl, Alfred and Gerald each had over 1,000 yards in their specialties—Gerald in receptions and Alfred in rushing.

As a high school student, Alfred Anderson wanted to be a quarterback on a college team and then play on a professional team someday. I felt that Alfred could be a great college quarterback but could be even greater as a running back. I could foresee him in the pros as a running back but not as a quarterback. On numerous occasions I sat down and talked with Alfred about this. I explained my thinking to him, but trusted him to make the final decision.

By his junior year it was decision time for Alfred Anderson. He had to decide whether he wanted to be a quarterback or a running back. I again explained my reasoning to him. I knew that it ran contrary to that deep burning desire inside him to play quarterback. He looked at me and said, "Coach Teaff, I believe you and know you have my best interests at heart and I, without question, intend to follow your suggestions and play running back. And I want you to know that I will be the best running back that I can possibly be." His being named All-Conference and a high pro draft choice, and now the success he has had in his rookie year, have been gratifying proof to both of us that Alfred made the right decision. It's a great feeling when expectations mesh and become a reality.

A Loss of Confidence

Gerald McNeil was the type of fellow who exuded confidence. That confidence had always helped him overcome his diminuitive size. I often told folks that Gerald thought he was 6-foot-6 instead of 5-foot-6. He certainly played like he was a much taller player.

In 1982 Gerald had an unusual slump. He was our punt return man and an extraordinary one at that. Suddenly, out of the blue, he began to mishandle the punts. I watched in horror as his confidence waned day by day. Then an incident occurred that really alarmed me. After mishandling two punts in the Texas Tech game, he came to the sideline and said he didn't want to handle the third punt. I knew that his confidence had been shattered, and that we were facing a serious problem.

We won that ball game anyway. It was my 100th major college victory and put me in an elite category, with the top ten current coaches who have won 100 or more major college games. Though excited and pleased about this victory, I was deeply troubled about what was happening to Gerald. I had seen him lose his confidence seemingly overnight and I knew that something had to be done to help him regain it quickly.

On Monday following the game, I watched Gerald practice and saw him drop three or four punts. I called him over to the sidelines, put my arm around him and asked him to come to my office to see me the next morning. When he arrived at my office, I told him that I believed he was having problems with his confidence in handling the ball. Confidence is something that we can control ourselves, I told him. I told him further that I wanted him to start right then to rebuild his confidence. Maybe for the first time, Gerald recognized the link between his talent on the football field and his personal mental attitude of confidence. I reminded him how important confidence is for a punt receiver. When a player is out in front of 50,000 people, with the lights glaring down into his face and sometimes the wind and rain clouding his situation, confidence in oneself is as important as one's talent in catching the ball.

I had some tapes on building confidence in my desk drawer, and I loaned these to Gerald. I asked him to listen to them every night for a week. I told him that we were starting right that minute to rebuild his confidence.

The next day in practice I set up some drills which were designed to help rebuild Gerald's confidence. Gradually, as the week progressed, I could see that Gerald was beginning to feel better about himself. The critical moment came in the next game, when the time arrived for Gerald to handle a punt. Did he do it correctly? Of course he did! With 50,000 people watching and cheering, Gerald returned that punt for 35 yards. He was well on his way to rebuilding his confidence. He never suffered a relapse after that, as his record all the way into the pros indicates. Not too long ago I watched on TV as Gerald returned a punt for a touchdown. As he crossed the goal line, I was proud of him and pleased that he had learned to face tomorrow's challenges with confidence.

Both Alfred Anderson and Gerald McNeil are now playing professional football. Gerald had an outstanding season in 1984 with the Houston Gamblers. Alfred Anderson was the NFC rookie of the year in 1984 for the Minnesota Vikings. Each man has a bright future, and they both have learned the importance of confidence—confidence in themselves and confidence in others.

The Power of the Intangible

Besides self-motivation, one of the key ingredients in my coaching philosophy is teaching a player to recognize the power of his intangibles. Intangibles are the innate, invisible characteristics that human beings possess. The list includes desire, confidence, loyalty, attitude, character, determination, faith, love, tenacity and the capacity to set goals and deal with rejection. Looking back over my coaching career, I can think of hundreds of examples of fine young men who learned to develop one or more intangibles that would propel them to success.

Attitude

Mark Adickes was one such young man. He was a sophomore on our 1980 championship team, but he suffered a serious knee injury during the first game that year, against Lamar University. He already had a rather obscure beginning with our team. He was not highly recruited. He was not all that big, only about 220 pounds and 6-foot-4. He had played football in high school in Germany for one year before moving to Killeen, Texas, where he continued to play ball. Then he was injured in 1980, just as our team's fortunes were beginning to blossom. He missed the entire 1980 season.

Many men would give up under such circumstances! But not Mark Adickes. He had that tenacity to keep on fighting when the odds were all against him.

With dogged determination that said, "I will not be whipped," Mark Adickes fought the long battle back to rehabilitation. Day after day he worked to rebuild the strength in his knee. I know it was painful for him. But he kept on fighting. By his senior year, he was not only All-Conference but he was also the best offensive lineman in America. He has now parlayed that desire to play into dollars. His bonus for signing with the Los Angeles Express was a cool one million dollars. That was in addition to his salary.

Ironically, he was injured again during one of the first games of his rookie year. It was another terrible knee injury. And again, Mark Adickes had that attitude that says, "I will not be defeated." It drove him to rehabilitate himself and return to the playing field again.

Desire and Determination

When a person has those intangible characteristics of desire and determination, there is not much that seems impossible to him. Sometimes it is sad to see such determination in a person who does not have the physical talent to do all that their heart desires. But even when that occurs, things work out.

One such person was Michie White. Michie lived in Venezuela with his family until his junior year in high school. He then moved to Mansfield, Texas, where he began to play American football. He had a great desire to play on the college level. He was not very big, certainly not very fast, but he was extremely intelligent and determined.

Michie had the proper mental attitude for success. But he

didn't have the football talent to get beyond the college level. Nevertheless, his pursuit of football and the development of his positive mental attitude did much for him.

Michie came to Baylor as a walk-on. He had to work hard to earn a scholarship. He finally got to play in the Rice game in 1982. But more importantly, Michie developed the power of the intangibles which now will help him the rest of his life. Today, at 24, Michie owns his own company and is heading toward a life of self-fulfillment and prosperity.

Learning to Deal with Elusive Goals

One of the most important aspects in playing the game is learning how to handle whatever comes one's way. Not only do the walk-ons have to learn to deal with defeat, rejection and failure, but the highly recruited student athletes also must learn to handle these problems. The outcome of their college football careers really depends upon how they, as individuals, handle their own skills and motivations and how they set their priorities and how they deal with what they have been given. I have seen players literally disintegrate, actually falling apart and dropping out of school because they could not handle the peaks and valleys in their lives. I have seen other players use what they have been given and turn into successful, outstanding men in the community.

One doesn't have to become a superstar athlete to learn how to use his ability and talents.

Phil Massey was a highly sought-after quarterback from Memphis, Tennessee. In 1980 I flew to Memphis to personally sign him. I immediately fell in love with his parents and knew I had a special young man to work with for the next four years. Phil Massey graduated in the spring of 1984 from Baylor University. Though he was a scholarship athlete, he spent four years on the scout team and played briefly in only two games. But Phil was not one to complain or become defeated. He became a leader on the scout team. Not one time in four years did he ever say one critical thing nor did he portray negative feelings or emotions toward our program or individuals involved in our program.

Phil Massey is a winner, because he used his intangibles to become the person he was meant to be. He became an outstanding student. He worked with youth groups around Waco, and he was looked upon by all the members of the team and the coaching staff as a truly outstanding human being. Phil came by my office just the other day to thank me for the opportunity he had of being a part of the Baylor program. I will miss Phil as much as I will any young man who made All-American for us.

Loyalty Makes a Difference

Coaches, as well as players, have played a special part in my life. I have learned much more from them than I have taught.

Coaches come in two categories, those who are working to become head coaches, and those who are committed to growing where they are planted. It is great that in coaching we can fall into either category and do what we love to do—work with young people in their total development.

I have ten former associates who have been head college coaches. Then, there are men like Cotton Davidson, Bill Lane and Wade Turner, whose total time in coaching with me equals 48 years. These men have invested their lives with me at Baylor.

Every coach I have been associated with has different strengths in terms of his intangibles, but they all possess one that is essential—loyalty.

Using What God Has Given You

Our society is caught up in winning. Our sports industry is obsessed with winning. Our business community is determined to win, too. Everything seems to be measured by that bottom line of wins versus losses. I still believe a person can be a winner without winning numerically every time he is engaged in competition. You become a winner based on what you do with what God has given you.

Circumstances sometimes control whether we win or lose, but we control whether we are winners or losers.

In 1972, when I was new to the Baylor University campus, a group of students came by my office and asked if I would make a statement that they could incorporate into a tract to be distributed at the upcoming game against Texas A&M University. I wrote that tract for them. It was titled, "The Difference at

Baylor." My point in that tract was that Baylor is a Christian institution and winning is more than just the final score on the scoreboard. I listed the Four Spiritual Laws and said that it is not so important whether one wins or loses but how one plays the game. If a person has Jesus Christ as his personal Savior, he will be a winner. If he does not, he will be a loser.

Some hours before the game, several of my assistant coaches found some of the tracts. They were worried that the tract would be misunderstood as an excuse for us to lose. I said I had no intention of losing that game, but that I was trying to drive home an important point about life.

We won that game in both areas. The scoreboard showed the final score of 15–14 in favor of Baylor. But more importantly, we had the chance to tell others about the way to really win. I never heard from one person that night who read one of those tracts. No one ever told me that because of that tract he or she turned his or her life over to the Lord.

Then almost twelve years later, in April, 1985, I flew to Amarillo to speak to a group of Baptist men. I was met at the airport by Richard Mason, a young man who played on our 1972 team. In the car on the way back to the airport after the talk, Richard told me something that will forever remain with me. "Coach, when you came to Baylor in 1972 I was not a Christian," he said. "But because of your faith and the things you tried to teach us, I came to know Christ. It has made a tremendous difference in my life. I now have the opportunity to work with people and to be in a position of responsibility in my church. I have a beautiful family and a Christian home."

Richard Mason's team in 1972 was 5–6. In the eyes of the world, they were losers. But without question, in the eyes of God and the true definition of the word, Richard is a winner.

It's How You Play the Game

Doug McCuen will never play for me, although he wanted to. He will never graduate from Baylor University, although he wanted to. Doug will never play professional football although he wanted to. Doug died March 26, 1985.

Doug's name used to be Russell, the name given him by his birth family. Russell was abandoned at an early age. Then he became part of a loving, caring family through adoption. His new father taught him to fish and encouraged him to participate in sports. Russell was good and by the time he was a sophomore in high school he weighed 200 pounds.

Russell loved his adopted father, Doug McCuen. When he was in junior high school, Russell started telling everyone he wanted to be called Doug. This was his way of saying that even though he was adopted, he was Doug McCuen's son.

Doug's best friend, Derrick McAdoo, came to Baylor to play football, and so eventually Doug became a part of the Baylor family, too. During his sophomore season, Doug's knee began to bother him. When the doctors X-rayed the knee they found a dark spot on the bone that was cancerous. The fierce battle had begun, and Doug was a real fighter. Doug thought he could lick it. He became the shining light of hope and inspiration at M. D. Anderson Hospital in Houston. Many times Doug would drive across town at a doctor's request to encourage another cancer patient.

Doug lost his leg, but kept on fighting. He lost the muscle tone he had worked so hard to develop, but he kept on fighting. Doug came to several Baylor football games to watch Derrick McAdoo play, and we became friends. Doug was in a wheelchair and weighed less than 100 pounds, but he had a great attitude.

In mid-February, 1985, Derrick called me at home to inform me that Doug was deteriorating fast and that he wanted to see me. I called Doug, and he was in good spirits as always. I tried to explain to him how busy I was. "You know Doug, recruiting, Nike meetings. Southwest Conference meetings, and so forth," I said. I told him I would come down the first week of March. Doug paused a moment and in a clear voice said, "Coach, I don't think I'll be here in March." I told him I'd be there on Sunday. He said, "Great."

Sunday, February 24, 1985, will be a day I will long remember. Baylor secondary coach Rick Johnson and I flew to San Antonio to speak to the Franka Football Clinic. We then flew to Houston where Doug's dad picked us up at the airport and drove us across town to their home. The pain that this father was feeling was shielded by the obvious love he had for his special son.

When we arrived at the home, Rick and I went upstairs to

Doug's room. I was not prepared. Doug had lost a lot more weight and was experiencing some breathing problems. Rick left the room, and Doug sat up in his bed. I knew this was the last time I would see Doug and he knew it as well. He showed me pictures of his sister and mother and a very special fishing trip with his dad.

He said, "I hope they know how much I love them and what their love has meant to me." Doug leaned up against the headboard of the bed and said, "Coach, do you think Derrick will start? Stay on him, Coach. He can be great." I smiled at the wisdom of that statement, then changed the subject of the conversation. "Doug, I have been told that you have shared your faith with a lot of young people." He said that he had and that he would continue as long as he could.

Two hours passed quickly, and it was time to go. I stood and extended my hand. As we looked into each other's eyes, he said, "Coach, I'm going to lose this fight, but I'm not a loser. I'm a winner."

Doug died one month later.

Winning
Is in the way you play the game each and every day.
It's in your attitude and in the things you say.
It's not in reaching wealth or fame.
It's not in reaching goals that others seek to claim.
Winning is having faith and giving confidence to a friend.
It's never giving up or never giving in.
It's in wanting something so badly you could die.
Then if it doesn't come, be willing to give it one more try.
Winning is being clean, and sound of mind;
It's being loyal to and serving all mankind.
Winning is in your teammates, friends, family and what they learn from you.
Winning is having character in everything you do.
Winning . . . it's how you play the game.